D0853906

William M. Timpson (Ph.D., educational psychology, University of Wisconsin) found that his participation in music and dance productions greatly benefited his teaching at an inner-city school where morale and achievement were low. He now puts his findings to work as a member of the education faculty at Colorado State University.

David N. Tobin (Ph.D., English literature, Princeton University), a member of the humanities faculty at Oxford College of Emory University in Oxford, Georgia, augments his teaching with considerable experience in the theater, both as an actor and a director.

Teaching as Performing

A Guide to Energizing
Your Public Presentation

William M. Timpson
David N. Tobin

A SPECTRUM BOOK
PRENTICE-HALL, INC., Englewood Cliffs, NJ 07632

Library of Congress Cataloging in Publication Data

Timpson, William M., date
    Teaching as performing.

    "A Spectrum Book."
    Includes bibliographical references and index.
      1.   Teaching.   2.   Expression—Teacher training.
3.   Performance art—Teacher training.   4.   Oral communication—Teacher training.   I.   Tobin, David N.   II.   Title.
LB1731.T55   371.1'22   81-15682
                                      AACR2

ISBN 0-13-891382-X

ISBN 0-13-891374-9 {PBK.}

Editorial/production supervision and interior design
    by Louise M. Marcewicz
Cover design by Judith Kazdym Leeds
Manufacturing buyer: Cathie Lenard

This work was developed under a grant from the Department of
Education. However, the content does not necessarily reflect the
position or policy of that Agency, and no official endorsement of
these materials should be inferred.

10 9 8 7 6 5 4 3 2 1

PRENTICE-HALL INTERNATIONAL, INC., *London*
PRENTICE-HALL OF AUSTRALIA PTY. LIMITED, *Sydney*
PRENTICE-HALL OF CANADA, LTD., *Toronto*
PRENTICE-HALL OF INDIA PRIVATE LIMITED, *New Delhi*
PRENTICE-HALL OF JAPAN, INC., *Tokyo*
PRENTICE-HALL OF SOUTHEAST ASIA PTE. LTD., *Singapore*
WHITEHALL BOOKS LIMITED, *Wellington, New Zealand*

Contents

Preface

All of us, not just teachers, are performers at one time or another, and we could all benefit from some training in performance skills. This book is not only an introduction to the idea of teaching as one of the performing arts but also a guide to energizing almost any kind of public presentation, whether it be in the classroom or the conference room.

The performing arts contain a rich body of literature and experience for teachers of any kind, at any level. Both stage performers and teachers are involved in the difficult process of communicating with an audience, and they both have mind, body, and voice at their disposal. Much of the performer's skills and training are highly applicable to the needs of the teacher, yet very little has been written that brings together these two related endeavors. Of course, effective teaching does demand much that is a long way from what we think of as "theatrical," but it also benefits from flexibility, variety, spontaneity, humor, energy, and enthusiasm. *All* of these presentational qualities are cultivated in the study of performance.

Ours is not a crash course in the wonders of superficial showmanship. None of the methods we discuss will ever come close to replacing the simple requirement of knowing one's field well. But with that knowledge as the essential foundation, teachers can go on to learn much from the performer.

Far too many people assume that the realm of the performing arts, particularly acting, is a secret domain cut off from all but those who are either fanatical devotees or frustrated hams. This book demonstrates both the easy accessibility and the wide applicability of these crafts. Learning about acting, for instance—about how to make full use of your body, face, voice, and feelings in order to express whatever needs to be expressed—is something obviously not limited solely to work on a stage. It applies to countless aspects of our lives, and it is open to all who want to explore some of those potentials that have been too often neglected.

Many of our suggestions and conclusions have been developed not in the study but rather in various workshops and classes on teaching as performing. Still, the book is flexible enough to be used either as the basis for a formal class or in a more individualized self-help format. Many of the learning activities require the participation of a group or at least one other person; other exercises require only a single open mind.

After an introductory justification of our views and description of the workshop out of which this text grew, we move on to interviews with actors and teachers who have confirmed the significance of our approach. Then follow chapters on specific components of the performer's instrument: body, hands and face, and voice, with complementary material on the value of pantomime and the importance of mustering and controlling energy. At this point, we start to focus on improvisation and other activities that will allow readers to make use of what they have already learned or are still learning. Finally, we turn to selections from works that present various points of view about teaching while at the same time providing good raw material for more performance work.

Regarding teaching as one of the performing arts is an approach both unorthodox and unexplored; therein lie its challenges as well as its rewards. New territory like this is hard to find. Let us be resourceful explorers.

We want to thank the institutions and, more important, the people whose help and inspiration were essential in the development of this book: Dr. Bill Smith, former national director of Teacher Corps; the Teacher Corps program at Colorado State University; Bill Johnson, Jim Kincaid, and Barb Nelson, encouragers of creative activities such as this; Christine Buster and the dance company at East Cleveland Community Theater; the colleagues and students of Patrick Henry Junior High School and the Cleveland Job Corps Center; Bob Davidson and Frank Farely of the University of Wisconsin at Madison; Jan Quintana, who typed and retyped the manuscript; the television production crew in the Office of Instructional Services at CSU, who helped us develop the excellent videotapes that accompany this training; the casts of *The Mikado* and *Oklahoma!,* produced in Fort Collins, Colorado, as well as the Festival Choir and the Larimer Chorale; the teachers who have participated in our training and given us what we can now share with others; Dianne Waters and David Pendleton, both of whose acting experiences showed us valuable perspectives; Miriam Berry, memorable teacher of music; the late Daniel Seltzer of Princeton University, actor-teacher par excellence; the Academy Theatre of Atlanta, Georgia, particularly the company of *Richard III* and its director, Leo Shapiro; and the cast of Oxford College's production of *The Glass Menagerie*— David Denholtz, Ellanor Pruitt, Mac Sitton, and Laura Susan Smith.

Dedicated to our friends, our families, and those teachers who have survived disillusionment and still believe that what they are doing in the classroom is important enough to work at and improve.

chapter one

Introduction

We are all performers. The boss who is never satis-fied with the productivity of his employees and winds up scowling constantly, the worker who tries to look busy to avoid additional chores, the young parent who needs to remain calm and responsive after seemingly endless hours with a bawling infant, the child who pouts and sulks when denied that life-sustaining cookie, the politicians who must at least appear to be pub-licly responsive to the needs of their constituents—all these people perform, whether consciously or uncon-sciously. There is also the student who must appear attentive to avoid some dull instructor's wrath, or the teacher who needs to maintain enthusiasm for students who don't care or for a course that has lost its appeal through endless repetition, or the administrator who must appear calm despite too many interruptions and crises. What is common to all of these is, in part, performing: appearing to be that someone you need to be at a particular moment.

"Hypocrisy," cry critics of this point of view, "deceit, whitewash, superficial razzmatazz." They insist that what we need in the educational field are genuine, down-to-earth people, not exhibitionistic cheerleaders and jugglers. The dawning of our age of Aquarius supposedly had rid us of that social straitjacket of conformity, allowing individuals to grow into the full bloom of self-actualization. "Schools are not meant to be circuses," they maintain.

In a now classic educational experiment, an actor was hired to masquerade as one Dr. Fox and deliver to a graduate-level class a lecture full of energy, wit, drama, anecdotes, and asides, yet devoid of real substance and even contradictory in places. When this Dr. Fox was later evaluated by his audience as a dynamic lecturer, the experimenters concluded that students can be snowed: they can confuse show with substance.[1] Other research, while recognizing the overlap between teaching and entertaining, has confirmed that highly rated teachers focus on substance and that sheer entertainment is not what most students see as good teaching.[2]

---

[1]See D. H. Naftulin, J. E. Ware, and F. A. Donnelly, "The Doctor Fox Lecture: A Paradigm of Educational Seduction," *Journal of Medical Education* 48 (1973):630–35.

[2]See E. R. Guthrie, *The Evaluation of Teaching: A Progress Report* (Seattle: University of Washington Press, 1954); see also F. Costin, W. T. Greenough, and R. J. Menges, "Student Ratings of College Teaching:

(Of course, teachers are not in the entertainment business. Yet the requirements for effective instruction do include enthusiasm, variety, flexibility, sensitivity, and humor.[3] Granted, education is a very human process; how then do we get people to change—to be more varied, flexible, and sensitive? This is exactly why teachers must study the skills of performance: both to understand better what they themselves are doing and to have some system for improvement. To accomplish this, teachers must also be students. And educators of teachers have been sorely remiss in providing them with the means by which to take on that role.

We must, however, go further than just saying this is what teachers need to be; they must be given the means to attain these skills. In his popular cookbook for success, *Teacher Effectiveness Training,* Thomas Gordon calls for changes: teachers need to model or project what they value and to modify themselves to be more accepting. Perhaps even more important, in Gordon's view, teachers need to overcome their traditional timidity and assert more controls over their own profession.[4] But just how does one go about doing this? How do we analyze what we presently do? How do we change? Unfortunately, Gordon gives no clues beyond the general directive. And so it is with most prescriptions for change: even if we could all

Reliability, Validity, and Usefulness," *Review of Educational Research* 41 (Dec. 1971):511–35.

[3]See K. E. Eble, *The Craft of Teaching* (San Francisco: Jossey-Bass, 1976); J. A. Centra, *Determining Faculty Effectiveness* (San Francisco: Jossey-Bass, 1979); N. L. Gage, ed., *Handbook of Research on Teaching* (Chicago: Rand McNally, 1963); and R. M. W. Travers, ed., *Second Handbook of Research on Teaching* (Chicago: Rand McNally, 1973).

[4]Thomas Gordon, *T.E.T.: Teacher Effectiveness Training* (New York: P. H. Wyden, 1974).

agree about the direction, we are at a loss over how to get there.

While teachers generally receive strong preparation in the subject matter of their fields, few are taught much about techniques of concentration and relaxation; about presentation and delivery; about voice, movement, and timing. All these skills, which professional performers study so assiduously, educators seemingly take for granted. As a result, those who are "natural" or "born" teachers can survive and flourish; those with instincts less theatrical often sink into mediocrity, or worse.

Good teaching requires much beyond knowledge of a subject; presentational skills are just as important. While professors of education will lecture about the components and varieties of effective instruction, they do little to assist teachers in developing anything beyond an awareness of ideals. There is, in other words, no practical training in this area. As a consequence, teaching styles are often out of sync with instructional objectives. Teachers' behavior in the classroom becomes more a by-product of survival than a function of conscious design and development.

We are not arguing for "hype" over substance; of course we need teachers who are not only articulate but also well trained and knowledgeable in their fields. We also need teachers who care about kids and learning. But what about those Monday-morning blues, or Friday-afternoon big-game crazies, or February blahs? What about apathetic students and a dull curriculum? With the training of the performer, teachers will possess skills to help overcome these obstacles and create the kinds of moods and learning environments they want.

These skills will also help teachers to conquer

inhibitions that limit their effectiveness. Developing potential requires the taking of risks. Every performer we have talked to stresses the importance of risks in building confidence and stretching capacities (see chapter two). Yet, many teachers are conservative in nature; they are not prone to flamboyance. Compound this with the fact that most people become inhibited when they have to be in front of others (the chief obstacle to truthful acting), and you have some serious barriers to risk taking.

Webster's defines inhibition as "something that forbids or debars; an inner impediment to free activity, expression, or functioning." The impediments are in part physiological. We commonly refer to someone "clutching" at the big moment, or "choking," and these terms are literally true. A muscular constriction occurs when we perceive an external threat. This "tightening" is a natural protective response the body uses to defend itself, and it is a very real phenomenon. Movements become shorter, quicker, and much more limited in scope. The voice rises. Add the adrenalin that typically accompanies this "flight or fight" reaction, and the result is a whole array of what the audience perceives to be nervous mannerisms or expressions: shifting your weight, fiddling with your hands, interposing "um's" and "ah's" and "you know's," darting your eyes, speaking too fast. Studying movement and other performance skills (such as warming-up techniques) will enable you better to sense these half-conscious or unconscious responses. Once you become *aware* of them, you will be able to control them.

Another problem related to inhibitions is stress. There is no question but that teaching is a highly stressful profession. American ideals about schools as melting pots and vehicles for equal opportunity seem to clash on a nearly daily basis with the classroom realities of the social class structure, economic inequities, handicaps and disabilities, and traditions of prejudice and discrimination. Teachers are on the front lines of that struggle.

Physiologically, stress has some profound effects. Internally, ulcers and high blood pressure are common by-products; externally, the results include sleeplessness and exhaustion. Although most of us have less severe symptoms, often only in response to specific situations, there are many still bothered by tight, sore neck and shoulder muscles, or back problems. While we may not realize it or want to admit it, the culprit is often stress, and stressful situations in teaching are endless. Because of the need to get some exams returned quickly, for instance, we sit bent over long into the night. Not having sufficient time to prepare for a particular day leaves us "under the gun" to come up with something. Being at the low end of the professional's salary ladder keeps us in a seemingly constant state of worry.

To combat stress we need to be able to recognize its symptoms. Studying movement and acting will put you in closer touch with yourself. You will become more conscious of the body and voice as instruments that need tuning and care, and that can be a lot more helpful than you had imagined. Keeping yourself in good physical condition and warming up before class will help control and dissipate the biochemical energy that stress builds up in your body.

Study of performance skills will also enable you to be what you need to be on a particular day, for a particular class or student. If a Friday comes along on which getting through the day seems impossible, then use the technique of "mounting" enthusiasm on your-self in class: imitate its physical manifestations. Walk faster and with more intensity, speak in a more varied and louder voice, make some grand gestures. By working yourself up, even though you really do not feel like it, you will force your body to pump the necessary adrenalin into your system. The additional adrenalin will soon make you feel more energetic. Or use your memory and recall a time when you were excited. With concentration, you can let that experience rejuvenate you. Or do something totally unex-pected: surprise the class with a shout or a whisper or a silence; talk to them as you would to a group of friendly acquaintances. Show them that, despite the necessities of scheduling, you are *not* an entirely predictable automaton. The element of the unexpected is an essential part of performing, and consequently of teaching.

We have tested our ideas over several years and with diverse audiences. The program "Teaching as Per-forming" has been presented in different forms: one-to three-hour presentations, complete workshops, and graduate courses. We have worked with instructors at all levels: primary and elementary schools; middle, junior, and senior high schools; colleges and univer-sities. We have enrolled undergraduates prior to their student teaching. We have also attracted many people from outside the teaching profession, such as youth-group counselors, social workers, and police. The response has been most encouraging, which is why we decided to write this book.

   In a recent class on teaching as performing, a rather timid biology professor explained why he was interested in these skills. As a researcher, he had been trained for careful and methodical pursuit of new knowledge, and he truly loved what he did. But to large classes of undergraduates, his quiet demeanor appeared to reflect boredom on his part. Of course, this interfered with his being an effective instructor, and he sought our assistance. How could we help him to convey his love for biology to his students?

Other examples of people who have taken this class will help to illustrate both the extent of the problem that our approach addresses and the potential diversity of the audience. An undergraduate in a teacher certification program was uncertain of her skills and wanted some training prior to student teaching. A first-year teacher felt he was being taken advantage of; he wanted some help in being more assertive in class. A veteran teacher came looking for a way to rejuvenate herself, to rekindle the spark that had been nearly extinguished by years of teaching the same old stuff. An academic counselor on campus wanted some fresh ideas for motivating her advisees. A veterinarian found that his lecture delivery was flat and that he was losing part of his audience. Another professor was there partly under pressure from his department chairperson to do something to improve his teaching. Some professors sought help in finding the right balance between too little and too much humor. Others always knew they were acting at times, but were interested in some formal training. A counselor in the Campfire Girls program lacked confidence in her ability to be effective at the numerous meetings she was called upon to address. A police officer enrolled to improve his ability to deal with the public, an increasingly critical aspect of modern police work. Thus, the appeal for this kind of training is indeed far-reaching. But because it involves a hybridization of several disciplines—education, theater, speech, and voice—few are presently prepared to offer it.

The workshop training has proceeded in four stages. First, class members are asked to take over and teach a few classes on something unrelated to their professional responsibilities. By drawing upon their own hobbies and interests outside of the classroom, individuals naturally radiate an excitement often missing from their more formal presentations. Through careful analysis of this fresh presentation, we begin to build an understanding and working knowledge of the energy and skills involved. We also establish a reference point for the future: an individual teacher can recall this special moment, physically and emotionally, as a way to enliven a lesson. Both of these techniques—careful analysis and reproduction of the required actions, and recall of past moods for use in the present—are known and practiced by performers everywhere (see chapter seven). The first is an external method (copying from the outside), the second internal.

Second, everyone is required to perform a brief pantomime. Given that teaching is primarily a verbal endeavor and that most classrooms are dominated (often excessively) by teachers' talk, pantomime is one activity that forces teachers in particular to become more aware of their nonverbal selves.[5] With that sensitivity, we can not only attack all those common, unnecessary gestures and mannerisms that often interfere with instruction, but also begin to amplify

[5]See A. A. Bellack, H. M. Kliebard, R. T. Hyman, and F. L. Smith, *The Language of the Classroom* (New York: Teachers College Press, 1966); J. Hoetker and W. P. Ahlbrand, Jr., "The Persistence of the Recitation," *American Educational Research Journal* 6 (March 1969):145–67; and N. A. Flanders, *Analyzing Teacher Behavior* (Reading, Mass.: Addison-Wesley, 1970).

the spoken message with appropriate movement. Because teachers rely so heavily on verbal communication, however, the pantomime itself is a quite difficult task.

Third, each class member must perform a dramatic reading. The objective here is twofold: to focus on vocal and facial flexibility, and to demonstrate how much can be done with the simplest of efforts, without memorization, elaborate costuming, or set. Watch a good primary school teacher read a story, and you will see the magic and power possible with this technique.

Finally, all is brought together into a culminating performance in which people are asked to become characters relevant to their teaching areas. For example, a professor of agriculture took himself and his audience to the year 2020 and played a young professor looking back on the primitive agricultural techniques of the twentieth century; a tutor portrayed the archetypal bad student doing homework (radio at full blast); a social worker played a client muddled with alcohol, something she wanted to understand in her job.

Along with these four stages, there is an accompanying and equally important routine. Every class begins with an exercise period. We stretch and bend and bounce while we talk about the importance of warming up. By focusing on the task at hand, teachers can stimulate physical flexibility while either relieving preclass tensions if they are nervous or enlivening themselves if they are blasé. Later, we add vocal exercise as well. Eventually, class members select a warm-up routine particularly suited to themselves.

Following this exercise period is the day's discussion. The tone is kept informal, and participation is encouraged as a way of continually building trust. Since we are asking everyone to undertake considerable risks in this class, the group as a whole must grow comfortable and supportive of each other. Following this the class is broken down into small groups of three to four persons for rehearsal and feedback. Each group then finds a quiet place to work, views each other's pieces, and offers suggestions for improvement. These pieces are rehearsed, refined, and polished; at least one performance from each group is presented before the entire class. This group activity is important for building trust and encouraging risk taking in a nonthreatening atmosphere. Feedback and rehearsal, of course, are absolutely essential for the development of skills.

Toward the end of the class, time is reserved for videotaping in a studio each individual's best performance. This not only preserves a record for future classes, but also motivates the students to perform at their best.

The training and retraining of teachers leave much room for improvement. Few teachers require assistance in the subject matter of their fields, except for periodic updating, which they know how to manage. But most *could* benefit from assistance related to their teaching styles, which are neither inborn nor immutable. They are, rather, functions of learning and experience, and consequently subject to change. As public figures, teachers rely upon the same skills that performers everywhere use. We must recognize this and accord the development of these skills an appropriate place in the curricula of our teachers, present and future. Let us consider the possibility that teaching is itself one of the performing arts.

chapter two

Points of View: Actor, Teacher, Director

We have talked to professional and amateur actors about the relationship between teaching and performing; this chapter presents a digest of their views. Although chosen at random, many of these actors turned out to have been teachers at one time or another, which is itself revealing. One taught high-school English for two years; another holds classes in acting and movement; an amateur actress we spoke to is a practicing nurse in labor and delivery who helps teach childbirth classes for first-time parents. One was a language tutor for a while, while another taught junior-high science in the inner city before committing himself to professional theater. They have been on both sides of the fence, and their perspective confirms the approach of this book.

First of all, they spoke of the parallels between acting and teaching. Both constantly exercise one's capacity to learn; both are problem-solving activities; both involve playing roles in order to communicate. "If you have thirty students, then you have thirty problems," says one former teacher. "You're constantly being confronted with problems—many of them stimulating—in the classroom and on the stage. Actors *have* to deal with them, but too often, teachers will avoid the problem. 'I'm supposed to be a teacher, not a disciplinarian,' they'll say. But the two can't always be separated. Acting class often boils down to being given a particular problem and having to solve it. There and then. All you've got are your own resources." Role playing is also important. One actress-teacher says, "The teacher must play the roles of supporter, evaluator, disciplinarian. And the teacher needs to choose different roles for different students if she's going to communicate. I perceive a certain student as especially sensitive, so *I* need to play a certain role that will fit the student."

Other parallels are just as obvious. "As an actor or teacher, you must know how to speak clearly and loudly enough for that back row," the nurse affirms. "Too many people assume that that comes naturally, but it has to be learned. And you have to *understand* what you are saying. If an actor doesn't fully understand the character he's trying to play, he'll be just as bad off as the teacher who walks into a class unprepared." Another actress sees this relationship to the material as more significant than the relationship to any audience. Whether it be a script or the day's lesson plan, the performer or teacher must know it inside out. This knowledge serves a kind of liberating function. The actor is free to concentrate on what is happening around him rather than on what his lines are, while the teacher is free to deal with questions and diversions instead of being locked into one particular approach.

The audience relationship, however, cannot be overlooked. "If you leave the audience out"—that is, if you are not aware of their responses and do not adjust accordingly—"then it's T.V." Teachers and actors stand alone and exposed to the critical multitudes, and the tendency is to work *too* hard: to give the audience everything instead of compelling them to participate in the process. In the theater this is overacting; in the classroom, what we will call "over-teaching." "One of the biggest mistakes I've made as an actress," says one, "is to work too hard to lay the character out in front of the audience so that they don't have to feel or do *anything.*" In one play her director insisted that she play a hysterical character by pulling out all the stops and being hysterical from beginning to end. "I noticed that the audience was actually sitting further and further back in their seats, and by the end I'm sure they were just as tired of the whole business as I was." She simply gave too much. The audience did not have to imagine parts of the character in order to complete it; the result was caricature. In another play, though, with a character just as extreme, she held back more, forcing the audience to "work," giving them more room to imagine and conclude for themselves what the character was about. In the final scene, this character unconsciously reveals herself to be both mad and murderous. "I *could* have done it hysterically, but instead I was quiet—emotionally as well as vocally. I kept more within, so that the audience had to notice signs and interpret what they meant. This time, they were moving forward in their seats. I was drawing them in." For another actor, who has worked with the classics of Molière and Shakespeare, overacting remains the principal problem. "Rather than trying to reveal everything about the character, you need to hold some of it inside. Overacting is showing *everything* and leaving nothing to the imagination." When playing Antonio in *The Merchant of Venice,* he dwelt on some of the thoughts and feelings Antonio would want to hide. "Watching someone overact is like seeing the Mona Lisa with a great big grin."

Overteaching also leaves nothing to the imagination. We talk about this elsewhere: the teacher does too much of the thinking and doing, and the students grow more and more passive. Figuratively, if not literally, they move further and further back in their seats and into themselves.

Students can often tell when the enjoyment has fizzled and a teacher would rather be somewhere else. Similarly, "that's the *first* thing that reads [comes across to the viewer] on the stage: when an actor doesn't really want to be there," according to an actress whose roles have ranged from Elizabeth in *Richard III* to Tweedle-Dum in a production of *Alice in Wonderland.* "There are also actors and teachers who are just exhibitionistic" and who do not care about those who are subject to the exhibition. "Students pick up on that; they see the flashiness for what it is. My best teachers were the ones whose techniques may have been poor but who made me feel as though they

really cared—as though what I did *mattered* to them."
There are such things as honest and dishonest acting.
If the actor is just pretending and his mind is somewhere else, the performance will be dishonest. Slick
and effective, perhaps, but dishonest. If he cares
about the audience and the play, however, and if the
role draws upon elements of the actor's "real" self,
then the performance will be honest.

Actors and teachers are both specialists in communication. "A lecture can be just as creative a
communicative event as a stage performance," says
one actor who also writes, directs, and teaches. (His
classes include high-school workshops in basic acting
skills and improvisation.) "I'm not talking about
'showboating,' either; I'm talking about the art of
conveying ideas." He points out also that teaching
and acting "are service professions—serving a community, serving human beings." The high visibility of
celebrities and their earnings makes us forget that
there are plenty of working actors "who are not in it
for the money." They act for some of the same
reasons that a dedicated teacher teaches.

Something else that both actors and teachers
must face is the problem of repetition: the same material taught over and over again; the same play done
night after night. How does one avoid the deadening
effect of routine? What can be done to make each performance new? "I need to be in touch with exactly
how I'm feeling on a particular night," answers one
actress. Her mood and thoughts are not going to be
the same every night, and she can draw upon that
variety and use it, if she is aware of it. "I'll go through
a kind of preshow ritual that occupies my body and
frees my mind: warming up physically, putting on
make-up, walking about the stage. I'll try to notice

what's different, or what I haven't seen before." She also tries to rid herself of expectations built from previous performances. And she listens when on stage. "You have to concentrate and listen to what's being said on stage if you want to keep it fresh," another agrees. (Teachers are familiar with the importance and the difficulty of attentive listening.) Different audiences can stimulate you with "different energies." The material itself can also be a source of renewal: if the script is strong enough, the performer can discover more and more in it. Surely the teacher's "scripts"—the fields of English, mathematics, history, etc.—are rich enough to yield new approaches to old topics. Finally, though, there are no panaceas. Some performers shrug their shoulders and acknowledge that, after a point, there is no escaping the boredom of a routine show.

The challenge of repetition comes even with experience—but what about problems and obstacles that apply particularly to the novice? What must people who decide to try some acting be prepared for? What must they work towards? "Self-confidence" was the answer we heard over and over again. "You cannot create until you trust yourself and are willing to take risks and possibly fail," says one professional. "Otherwise you'll be emotionally constipated. You just have to learn to trust your impulses in the attempt to be a believable human being." Formal training is not necessary for this: "Children are often the best performers because they're *natural*." They have the least cluttered access to their genuine impulses. "You have to get over the trauma of exposing yourself," adds an actress. And how did she overcome this obstacle? "I exposed myself." The consensus is that the newcomer must take a deep breath, swallow fear, and take chances that will probably lead to some failures and a bruised ego. Strangely enough, this kind of conditioning will make it easier to take risks. Failure won't be so threatening because it has already been tasted, and there may even be some bolstering successes along the way.

Learning how to concentrate on stage is important for self-confidence, since concentration brings control. The "technique of images," another term for emotional recall, helps with concentration. One actor gave an example from his role as the Duke of Clarence in Shakespeare's *Richard III*. Clarence has been imprisoned by his brother Richard in the Tower of London. In act I, scene 4, he describes to the prison guard a terrible nightmare he has just had, which expresses guilt over his own bloody actions in the struggle for political power:

> ... then came wandering by / A shadow like an angel, with bright hair / Dabbled in blood; and he squeak'd out aloud, / 'Clarence is come; false, fleeting, perjured Clarence ... / Seize on him, Furies, take him to your torments!'

To ready himself for this moment, the actor remembered a night in California, on a ranch, when he saw what seemed to be a ghost. "I focused on the image of that presence, or whatever it was, in the doorway of the ranch, and this brought on a whole flood of feelings and sensations that suited the moment in the Tower, psychologically and emotionally. Stanislavski [the great Russian actor-director-teacher] called it plugging into the subconscious." On nights when the technique worked, he was not pretending fear—he was experiencing it.

An actress in the same production spoke of the same technique. She played Elizabeth, the queen whose children are assassinated in the Tower. That role was a big risk for her. Having no children, she of course has never lost one, and she was worried that since this kind of grief was outside her own experience, she would have difficulty communicating it to an audience. "I'm very close to my nieces and nephews, so I used them as substitutes, imagining what it would be like to lose *them*." Still, this was not enough, so she drew upon a childhood image. "When I was a kid I had a favorite horse. It broke its leg in the middle of an ice pond. I found it dead with a rat hole in its stomach." She used that image to help evoke the right state of mind and soul. "Sometimes it worked, and sometimes it didn't."

Physical technique is something else the beginning actor must learn. "You have to understand your own body language more, become more aware of it," says the actor who played Clarence. "Take some classes in modern dance, or classical dance, or fencing." This will help with self-consciousness, which is another problem. The beginner must also accept the boring nature of some basic exercises on concentration, sense memory, breath control, etc. "Acting is a lot harder than it looks," another professional remarks. Half-hearted dabbling in performance skills will be just about meaningless. If novices are not serious about working hard, they will wind up embarrassed. Nothing more.

One actress summed up the trials of the beginner particularly well. "Trying and failing and being criticized hurt my feelings. Taking a risk that didn't work out made me not want to take more." But there was enough desire to continue. "You must be prepared to learn things about yourself that aren't all going to be good. You may discover that you're less creative than you thought, or less brilliant (when someone else needs to explain the script). Or you may discover that your experience with life hasn't been that broad, when you have a difficult time understanding and creating a character with different kinds of experience. It's the same problem teachers have when they are confronted with students who come from backgrounds really different from their own."

Those performers who have had considerable teaching experience also talked about how acting skills and techniques can help in the classroom. Of course, some of the benefits are applicable to far more than just teaching. Still, they need to be pointed out in order to make clear that we are not just talking about highfalutin theatrics. Here are some basic categories drawn from our conversations. These are all methods and capabilities that can be of great value to teachers, regardless of their histrionic talent or desire.

Warm-ups and Relaxation

The ability to be physically and mentally relaxed in stressful situations is an essential part of an actor's resources. Relaxation is achieved through all kinds of preperformance warm-up exercises. A few examples follow.

1. Sit, breathe deeply, and concentrate on the physiological aspects of breathing, or on a sound silently repeated to oneself, or on the color spectrum, imagining each color somewhere between the eyes.

2. Try some neck rolls, or head stands, or somersaults, or sun salutations (exercising the head,

neck, arms, and trunk as though you were worshipping the sun).

3. Recite tongue twisters until you get them right many times in a row.

4. Do stretching exercises (yoga is a good source for these). For instance: lying on your back, bring the legs all the way back over the head until your knees are close to touching the floor. In that position (not as hard to reach as it may sound), concentrate on your breathing.

5. Before the show or class begins, give yourself five minutes to be silent and alone. Breathe deeply, stretch your limbs, and then shake them out.

Figure 1. As a professor of microbiology and department chairman responsible for an ambitious program°of teaching research in both microbiology and environmental health, Dr. John Bagby must spend a fair amount of time pushing papers around his desk. He's found our suggestions on warm-up exercises very helpful for invigorating him just prior to teaching. The time he takes for this also allows him to get away from the telephone and concentrate on the lesson ahead: how he'll lead into it and make the transitions from section to section.

These exercises may sound like more trouble than they are worth, but actors swear by them and depend on them.

Concentration and Listening

Actors and teachers are expected to behave and speak naturally and clearly in an unnatural situation: in front of a group of spectators. They are faced with many distractions, whether these be a restless audience, a botched cue, or unexpected questions in class. Acting fosters the ability to concentrate, to remain focused on the character's actions and words in spite of the glaring lights and the coughing in the third row and the misplaced prop. (This holds for minor as well as major roles; in fact, the challenge is often greater for the small role, where there are more temptations *not* to concentrate.) Listening on stage requires a particular kind of concentration that comes with practice and experience. "It's forcing yourself really to hear what the other person is saying, word by word," one amateur actor says. "That's not nearly as easy or as obvious as it sounds, what with all the distractions. To silence those parts of your mind that are shouting about your own next line and how poorly the last scene went and the two friends in the audience, and just to listen and observe what's happening on the stage, physically and emotionally—that's an achievement."

Self-Confidence

Most of the actors we talked to affirmed that, despite the risks that fail, performing experience does build self-confidence. As long as one's expectations are not overblown, there will be enough successes. And we are not just talking about triumphant leading roles. One college teacher, who could carry a tune but had almost no voice training, took the plunge and joined a local singing group. "I had been in high-school band but never in a chorus of any kind. Suddenly I was trying to sing Beethoven's Mass in C Major with a hundred people. By the time of the concert I was still faking some sections, but I certainly made a lot more progress than I had thought possible." "Acting makes it much easier to be in front of groups," one actor says. After walking out on a stage, walking into the classroom may pose fewer threats.

Self-Awareness

Studying acting is a way to learn about oneself. That is good for anyone, not just teachers. For one thing, acting develops a kind of self-monitoring instinct that can help teachers: it "hones one's sense of presentation—the perception of how one comes across." It also teaches a willingness to break boundaries, to use the body more effectively, or to find a new awareness of one's own creativity.

Human Relations

"As an actor, I'm always dealing with the psychology of different characters. What's motivating him? What does she want? Why are these characters behaving this way? If I don't ponder these questions, I'm lost. And you find after a while that asking these questions develops a sensitivity to other people's behavior in real life—their needs, their reasons for acting the way they do. That's helped my teaching."

"The stuff of acting is human relationships, which are also a part of the best kinds of teaching." The relational work of acting benefits the student-teacher relationship.

A DIRECTOR'S POINT OF VIEW

Dr. Morris Burns, a professor at Colorado State University, has taught courses in theater arts and directed plays for sixteen years. He has also taught, with Dr. Timpson, a graduate course in teaching as performing. Summarized below, his eight categories, each of which distinguishes one aspect of the common ground where teaching and acting come together,

Figure 2. Dr. Morris Burns, assistant professor and associate director of speech and theater arts.

recall much of what our interviewed performers have said.

1. Physical, Mental, and Emotional Preparation.

Some actors demand solitude before going on stage; some stay calm by seeking out company; others will continue to review their lines even though they know them perfectly; still others try to focus their energies by doing a series of exercises. Although there is great variety in preperformance preparations among actors, what is common to each is a conscious, systematic approach before going on stage. Many teachers do take the time to review their plans or notes before the start of a class. Many others, however, would benefit from taking preparation more seriously and seeing it as an important effort towards achieving the desired emotional and physical levels needed to improve a particular lesson.

2. "Reading" an Audience or Class. - *know your when you get loud*

In the theater, a production is not a production until it is played to an audience. Similarly, the final test for any lesson or lecture must be its effect on the students. During performances, directors will attend to any signs that they are losing their audiences: is there much shifting in the seats or coughing that spreads like wildfire? If teachers can learn to decode similar warning signals in their classrooms, they will then be able to vary their tempo or movements or activities in an effort to recapture the attention of their students. Of course, educators have a significant advantage over actors: they are not tied to a specific script or direction. More teachers need to learn how to make the most of that fact.

3. Creating the Proper Environment Through Set or Classroom Arrangement.

For the director, a great deal of time and effort goes into designing and building just the right set for each scene. In fact, set designers are important enough to receive billing that is typically not far below the director's. For actors, the stage setting is an indispensable tool; they long for as many rehearsals as possible within the actual environment that will be used in performance. Many find that their characterizations are finalized only when they have the benefit of rehearsing in the completed stage setting with all the assembled props. We are all to some extent defined by our environments. Actors are trained to use their space effectively; teachers could undoubtedly do much more in and with theirs. For instance, seating arrangements can be varied. With all students out in front, the teacher has what is called a proscenium stage. With students on three sides, you have a "thrust" stage. And with students on all four sides, the teacher has a theater in the round. Each of these variations on the actor-audience relationship has its own set of strengths and weaknesses as far as productions are concerned. In the "thrust" or round, a greater intimacy exists between actors and their audiences, although eye contact and projection become more complex. Again, the teachers' advantage is that they can choose the design that best suits them, their students, and their scripts.

4. Becoming the Needed Character.

With respect to acting, this ability is an obvious one. For the teacher it may be less obvious, yet it is equally vital. When Burns is faced with yet another introductory lecture on the theater, he will be the first to admit that the challenge has waned over the years and that everyday problems tend to interfere with his ability to concentrate. So he must consciously find a persona that will be fresh and stimulating. In other words, he acts. Rather than being phony, that is a professional response to a particular need. Burns has also found himself approaching a totally new course with a certain amount of fear, even though he feels confident about his material. In that kind of situation he must tell himself that he is confident, and he must act in a confident manner. "I've gone over the material. I know it. I'm convinced of its validity." When he finally enters the classroom, Burns radiates assuredness. This is acting—and his students are the benefactors.

5. Getting the Most Out of a Particular Script or Subject Matter.

For the actor, the script has typically been completely prepared prior to rehearsal, and although there may be variation in the amount of direction given, there is still direction. It is up to the actor then to learn the lines within the context of that direction. Burns, however, always tells his actors to be aware of the script's potential: to capitalize on its strengths and to defend against its weaknesses. For the teacher, while the differences are significant, the similarities are equally substantial. Certainly teachers are in much greater control of their own scripts—they write, direct, and produce them. While actors rehearse and do so under professional direction, teachers are typically limited to one-shot productions—premieres and closings all in one period—with little or no feedback or time to adjust. Yet, teachers can also capitalize on the potential in their scripts. They can continually reexamine their material. They can also build on the strengths and defend against the weaknesses. Although the script does change from day to day, there are regular patterns in the organization of the classroom, the presentation of the material, and the interactions between teacher and students that allow for reexamination, rehearsal, and further development. New examples and fresh approaches can be experimented with. "Directional" help can be sought from colleagues as well as students. On the other hand, teachers as well as actors must beware of becoming bored with their scripts and losing the energy so necessary for successful performances.

6. Adding Appropriate Movement, Gestures, and Expressions.

Actors will spend weeks poring over the physical enactments of their characters. What does a particular character look like? How does the character move? Michael Chekhov, in *To the Actor*, suggests that actors actually visualize what their characters look like and abstract specific elements from those pictures: the arms and fingers; the legs, stance and walk; the angle of the head; the eyes and mouth; the chest and back. For actors, the study of movement fulfills the physical requirements of the script and also reveals much about the psychological attitude of their characters. For teachers, these lessons are equally relevant. Appropriate and energetic movements will add to the material and convey a certain excitement to students. Directors and actors work hard to provide physical variety as well as eliminate unnecessary or excessive movements. The actor wants to be sure that all movements are meaningful; so should the teacher. Economy of movement is central to presentational clarity and power. Study, attention to detail, direction, and rehearsal are essential to successful movement.

Be especially attentive to the use of your eyes. As a listener or viewer, eye contact with the speaker or performer adds an important personal dimension. With practice—and the mirror is an excellent tool—moods and emphases, rewards and concerns can also be conveyed.

7. Making Effective Use of Vocal Range and Potential.

One of the primary tools shared by actors and teachers is of course the voice. Given that words dominate so much of what occurs on stage or in the classroom and that actors receive extensive training in voice, it certainly seems that educators are remiss in not providing similar training for teachers. Vocal range, strength, and flexibility can add valuable variety, emphasis, and even drama to any lesson. Silence as well can prove valuable.

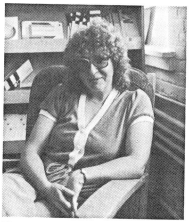

Figure 3. The workshop has enabled social worker Roseanne Cole to be more comfortable when talking to large groups of people. She's relaxed and more flexible; she can joke now. She's also become more conscious of her voice and mannerisms. Roseanne has become so successful in her presentations that she's been asked to help train prospective social workers.

8. Costuming.

As a director, Burns must pay critical attention to the costumes his characters will wear. Teachers should take note of this and attend more carefully to the effect their "costumes" have on their students. Again, variety may be important here. As the actor will experiment with the effect of particular costuming on an audience, so should the teacher.

Burns uses much from the theater in his own teaching. He finds it odd that educators have neglected to make the translation formal.

chapter three

The Body

We all move, and definite messages are conveyed by those movements, yet so many of us are not really very conscious of how our bodies telegraph signals. Americans in general, and American men in particular, tend to be uptight about both their physical nature and how they move. Find the most macho male you can and ask him to put on tights, join a dance class, and be graceful—and watch the horror as he rejects this affront to his masculinity. Male athletes who are quite accustomed to cavorting in public in scanty shorts maintain a strict double standard of what is permissible behavior on the court or field or in the locker room but not acceptable beyond. Contrast the style of dance in a gay as opposed to a straight bar; gay men are often less constrained by a need for a masculine image and much more relaxed, creative, and free in their movements.

Any competent actor will admit that all the sensitivity, feeling, and understanding in the world will be useless if the instrument of his body is not tuned and ready as a vehicle of communication. At least *half* of many actors' training is devoted to physical activity and the development of their physical resources through such disciplines as modern or classical dance, ballet, fencing, yoga, and calisthenics. In many cases, the actor preparing for the role of Hamlet or Lady Macbeth before each night's performance is *not* sitting in a dim corner backstage, dwelling on metaphysical questions of human suffering or ambition. Rather, he is loosening up his limbs and stretching his torso; she is doing some breathing exercises, thinking of muscular tensions and how to be rid of them. For both actor and teacher, a relaxed and expressive body is essential.

Not only with teachers, but with anyone working in front of a group, posture and movement convey definite messages to an audience. Is the speaker moving with confidence and ease or is he or she tensely clutching the lectern in some terrified death grip? Are the movements highly repetitive (for example, a nervous walk through an irrelevant though constant pattern)? Do the gestures have any relationship to the lesson at hand or are they merely personal mannerisms caused by a stressful situation—nervous responses that have become part of an unconscious routine?

All teachers and lecturers have certain mannerisms, many of which are unconscious effects of bodily tensions. Sometimes they do not seem to get in the way of the lesson or the message. On other occasions, however, these quirks become disasters. Students are distracted; they begin counting, charting, and anticipating each slip or twitch. One teacher was once told by a student that his habit of toying with a cigarette for a while before lighting it proved distracting to his audience. They began silently predicting how long he would take to light one. The teacher had thought those distracted gazes were from lack of interest. In fact, the students were quite interested—in cigarette manipulation.

We are not arguing for slick, robotlike delivery. Even good lecturers make mistakes and repeat nervous or routine patterns. But the vitality of their presentations, the strengths of their lessons, the meaningfulness of their courses, and their relationship with students outweigh the effects of inappropriate gestures or movements. In fact, these quirky mannerisms can help to make the already effective teacher more human in the students' eyes. It's when teachers are having difficulty getting their message across and the class is drifting that more of these mistakes seem to appear and interfere.

Most of us can look back through our own educations and discover examples of teachers who either misused their bodies or used them well. We remember a substitute teacher whose first entrance into the classroom—the manner in which this turkey strode up to his desk—let the students know immediately that they had a real loser on their hands and that it was open season on substitutes. Before he even opened his mouth, his awkward gait and stooped posture suggested that he could not fully control his own body,

Figure 4. Coauthor David Tobin believes in the importance of posture and body movement in gaining and holding the attention of a class.

let alone the class. On the other hand, many of us are also familiar with the teacher who is knowledgeable, articulate, entertaining, demanding, and animated, with a lively sense of how to make body and idea correspond. One teacher recalls a professor of European history. Twice a week, for an hour and a half at a crack, he would pace back and forth, reeling off dates and facts and trends ad infinitum, all embellished with just the right gestures. His timing was so precise that his movements perfectly matched the lecture. Frenzied periods in history were marked by short, quick steps and gestures; important events were emphasized by absolute stillness. Even though at that time the teller of this story had no intention of going into teaching, he was amazed at the professor's pedagogical perfection. Years later, he found out what time and effort went into perfecting each lesson. It was this information that, in retrospect, made the professor human: he had to work so hard to make his presentations look so effortless.

One very important book about movement in this context is *The Teacher Moves: An Analysis of Nonverbal Activity* (New York: Teachers College, 1971) by Barbara Grant and Dorothy Hennings. A number of teachers were videotaped and their movements analyzed. Approximately eighty percent of these teachers' movements were found to be related to the instructional process (that is, only twenty percent were nervous, personal irrelevancies). Over sixty percent of these movements involved conducting behavior (controlling participation or obtaining attention), approximately thirty percent involved wielding (moving toward action, picking up assignments, reading), but

Figure 5. Use of the arms and hands is important but often overlooked. Coauthor David Tobin cautions that gesturing *can* become distracting and silly if it's used thoughtlessly, but it can also be a valuable tool.

less than ten percent involved acting (emphasizing, illustrating, pantomiming, role playing, etc.). The authors concluded that much should be done to develop and expand acting gestures; otherwise, a tremendous instructional potential will continue to be wasted.

Specifically, Grant and Hennings recommend the following:

1. Eliminate contradictory cues. Too many teachers speak and act in a monotone while expressing "excitement" about a particular idea. Or the command "Think about it" is followed immediately by new material, allowing little if any time for actual contemplation.

2. Increase the right kind of nonverbal cues. To counteract the tendency of most teachers toward excessive verbosity, the authors suggest that we all look for opportunities to substitute nonverbal cues for verbal expressions. For example, pleasure over a particular response could be reflected in a facial expression or a hand gesture.

3. Eliminate irrelevant nonverbal cues. Given that some twenty percent of our teaching movements are personal (that is, have nothing to do with what is being taught), we all could benefit from an effort to minimize these. Idiosyncratic gestures or movements may be distracting.

EXERCISES

If you are to work on movement and improve your repertoire, there are important regular exercises and various experiences that will be helpful. The American physical tradition is a rather inflexible one, especially for males. Consequently, many of our teachers tend to be quite rigid in posture and are extremely limited in their knowledge of the kinds and amount of exercise and activity that can produce dramatic changes. Once again, it is primarily a matter of risk taking.

The following exercises are by no means the definitive collection. It's up to you to determine which are the most appropriate for you. However, it is important to have regular times set aside for exercising. Mornings are good because you can work away some of that sleep-induced stiffness. You'll find that as you get older, warm-ups become more and more essential prior to extended and intense periods of conditioning. But throughout the day, and especially just prior to class, you'll find that some stretching will reactivate and energize your system as well as give you some precious moments for focusing on what is ahead.

1. Become more aware of your posture. Stand erect, feet shoulder-width apart, knees slightly bent. Head up, eyes forward. Relaxed but alert. Be aware that "locked" knees cause much more fatigue than those that are slightly bent.

2. Start with the arms stretched out to the sides, parallel to the floor. Perform broad rotations from the shoulders, forward and backward. Repeat with smaller circles. Now rotate the wrists. Arms and wrists are important to exercise because of the tension that builds in our shoulders and the tiredness that develops in our hands from writing. Try rotating your arms and then your shoulders in opposite directions.

3. Now the neck. Move your head and neck in a

large circle, slowly, first to the right; then, after a couple of circles, to the left. Feel that tension begin to evaporate. Once relaxed, you'll be amazed at the versatility a loose neck can give you in expressing a wide variety of moods and reactions as well as in sensing when tension is building. Any good masseur will tell you how critical a relaxed neck is to the total relaxation of the body.

4. Now bend from the waist. First to the left, left arm by your side, right arm curved above your head and to the left. Shift your weight to the right so that you stretch that left leg. Just hang there. Don't bounce; relax. Now center your weight and slowly bend your upper torso forward, both arms at your sides. With each exhalation you should be able to sink further forward toward the floor. But keep your knees slightly bent so that you don't suffer unnecessary stress. Now swing to the right, left arm above your head and hooked to the right, your right arm down at your side, your body weight shifted left so that you stretch your right leg. Finally, center your weight and bend backwards, arms at your sides. These stretches are important because they release tension that builds in your back and spine.

5. Some swings: up on toes with arms stretched overhead, reaching; now swing your arms down toward the floor as you bend your knees. Then, back up on your toes, reaching, reaching, and down to the floor again.

6. Of course, if you want really to be serious, you have to get down on the floor and do a bunch of sit-ups. Firm up that middle! Roll over and do a

mess of push-ups. Strengthen those arms and shoulders! While stretching will get you relaxed and flexible, sit-ups and push-ups will make you stronger. The combination—relaxed, flexible, and strong—will make you unstoppable.

7. Loosely shake your arms and legs. Pretend that you're trying to throw away a hand or a foot. This

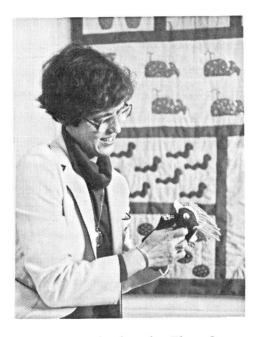

Figure 6. Preschool teacher Elaine Spencer seems to be using a great deal from our training. She has become more dramatic in her storytelling, and she does much more now with her voice. She has also taken to heart our recommendations about physical conditioning and joined with a few other teachers to exercise three times a week right after school. Now, she finds she has even more energy available for teaching. She does, however, have to be conscious of the energy level she brings to class; when her little people are already bouncing off the walls, she must consciously slow herself down.

is a common loosening-up exercise that actors use.

8. Explore the classroom when students are *not* there. Shout, jump around—use your body and voice in ways that are foreign to you. This increases your range and helps to break those inhibitions which can limit a teacher or actor. Try moving throughout the room. How do you feel? How does your voice sound?

Exercises like those above will set a positive physical and mental tone for your entire day. Any combination you do in preparation for each class will also set a tone, making each lesson something special. Your students will appreciate this, and you will in turn be reinforced by their reaction. It is energy that students respond to, and with a little work you can get all the energy you'll ever need.

chapter four

Hands
and Faces

Most of us have had little if any formal training in the performing arts, and what we know about acting is too often distorted by America's obsession with celebrity. Mention the word "acting," and for many you will bring to mind images of Hollywood, "stars," and *People* magazine. In addition, most people are exposed primarily to film and television acting, which are very different from the discipline of acting on the stage.

Despite many mistaken preconceptions about what acting is and what it involves, most of us do realize the obvious importance of facial expressions and related gestures. Still, when we get on the stage or in front of a class, the tendency is to shrink and tighten all of our movements, especially those of the face. Instead of becoming a compelling and infinitely varied organ of expression, the face deadens into a fixed mask. Controlled by one's nervousness instead of one's ideas, it has little to say.

What is the solution to this problem? The same that we will encounter over and over again: simply, increased self-awareness and a concomitant willingness to take risks. But beyond that, there are no easy or automatic formulae. Effective performances in the theater are quite varied, ranging from a broad style involving exaggerated gestures and expressions (often for a big auditorium) to a much more intimate, subdued manner (smaller theater).

Teachers need to experiment more and develop a greater repertoire of gestures and facial expressions. Research has demonstrated the positive effect of variety on learning;[6] the stock of various gestures and expressions is potentially one of our most abundant and accessible resources. Research has also shown that teachers tend to do too much of the talking that goes on in classrooms.[7] Gestures and facial expressions can be an eloquent means of nonverbal communication.

EXERCISES

With one person, go through each of the situations listed below, presenting your initial ideas, receiving feedback, and then modifying and repeating them.

[6]See note 3.
[7]See note 5.

Analyze each situation. Break it down into the component parts: fingers, hand and arm position and movement, mouth and lips, other facial muscles, eyes, angle of head, etc. Have a mirror handy to provide a second point of view.

1. A student gives a good answer. Instead of the usual response of "good," you give an A-O.K. sign (thumb and forefinger forming a circle) and make a face that indicates something tasty.

2. A slight disturbance arises in the back (where else?). You raise or turn your head quickly, hold and stare, eyebrows slightly raised in a questioning manner, and point.

3. Many of your students are having real difficulty with a particular problem or concept. Look puzzled as you confront the problem with them.

4. A colleague needs to talk, and you're really tired. Look like you're actively listening. (One benefit of "looking" like you are listening is that the energy needed for the behavioral characteristics of leaning forward and making appropriate gestures and facial expressions will eventually displace some of your tiredness and make it easier for you actually to listen.)

5. You need to be assertive with one of your administrators. Look the part.

6. You're disappointed with an entire class's performance.

7. You need to be angry with one particular student.

8. Perfect an "I don't know" shrug and look.

9. How about a "who me?"

10. Ever hug a student? Put a hand on a shoulder as you lean down to help? An arm around a shoulder as you walk and listen to a student's problem? Try them.

11. Point or nod to a student to answer.

12. When you need to be descriptive about someone or something, indicate:

huge	dainty	prayerful
wide	picky	defiant
tall	proud	lost
short	humble	cagey
narrow	shy	embarrassed
long	uncooperative	wrathful
bulging	gentle	fickle
clumsy	strong	

13. Express each of the emotions in point 12, one by one, in a mirror. Start off with each one naturalistically, then exaggerate more and more. Study the facial muscles and features closely.

14. Use your hands to emphasize the words and ideas of a popular song that you know.

15. Time out (hands perpendicular, forming a T). Count with your fingers for quiet.

16. Cup your mouth as if you were calling off into the distance: you are trying to "reach" two students who are having a conversation of their own.

17. Close your eyes tightly to protect yourself from the oncoming barrage of questions.

18. Clap your hands or snap your fingers to keep a pace going.

19. Squint your eyes as if you were looking into the wind or sun. This expression suggests attitudes ranging from puzzlement to dismay.

20. Flutter your eyelids to be cute (the heroine must reward her hero).

21. Express mock dismay over your students' clamorings for holding class outside on a beautiful day.

22. Come up with some gestures and expressions of your own.

chapter five

Pantomime

Now that we have considered bodily and facial movements, let us consider an art form that makes use only of them. The demanding art of pantomime requires physical flexibility and expressiveness, precise timing, stage presence (another term for *confidence*), and creativity. It is perhaps the most magical of the performing arts; audiences are eager to fall under the spell of masters like Charlie Chaplin, Stan Laurel, Claude Kipnis, and Marcel Marceau.

We are convinced that pantomime is one of the most important training and growth activities in which an instructor can engage. Why? Because teachers—

and this includes even the most dynamic—tend to interfere to some extent with the learning process by dominating the available time more than they need to. As we have already pointed out, research consistently demonstrates that teachers monopolize the talk time in a classroom. We often short-circuit the learning process by jumping in too quickly and too often with our own words; pantomime forces us to get along without them. Pantomime is one activity that forces instructors to look to their nonverbal talents for communicating.

What is both delightful and stimulating about pantomime is its attention to detail, its subtlety, and its requirement that viewers use their imaginations.

Figure 7. Already an accomplished musician, elementary music teacher Merry Manuel used our class to develop her storytelling techniques, illustrating various characters and events with a touch of pantomime. Her students are enjoying class more, and their recall has improved.

Movements and gestures are broken down into their elemental components, linked via a precise yet subtle choreography, and then displayed before an audience without props or costuming of any consequence. The viewer participates by "completing" the manifold images, and the effect can be marvelous.

For teachers and other beginners, however, the first attempts at pantomime typically result in the performer's feeling awkward, foolish, or downright terrified. We are part of a verbal society, and it's not just teachers whose lives are dominated by words. Moreover, we are also part of an uptight culture which severely limits the kinds and degrees of emotional and physical expressiveness that are acceptable. These factors make the pantomime both extremely demanding as well as absolutely vital to the teacher's process of growth.

In order to break into the rigors of pantomime, start with small sketches of everyday activities: waking up, dressing, brushing your teeth, opening and closing a door, driving a car, greeting an old friend or someone completely new, writing a letter, eating, drinking, undressing, getting back into bed. Attend to detail during your daily activities; *pay attention* to what you usually do automatically. Here's where an acute sense of observation and detail, one of the chief staples of acting classes, comes into play. When you first awake, do you look at the clock? Doze for a bit? Change position? Lie still with your eyes open? How do you get out of bed? Do you roll over toward the edge? Or sit up? Which leg goes out first? And how? Do you sit for a moment on the bed's edge or move quickly for the bathroom? Do you stretch? Rub your eyes? What sounds do you make? Is your walk a shuffle, a bounce, or that of a death-row inmate? How long or short is your stride? What expression is on your face, if any? Whatever your feelings, how are they expressed in your body, gestures, and expressions? Do you have a specific routine? Do you glance out a window first? Do you check out what the mirror might say that morning? When do you begin thinking of the day's wardrobe, of what you must do? And how do all of these elements change according to the amount of sleep you received, when you went to sleep and when you had to get up, the mood you're in now or were in the night before, how you survived the day before or how you'll get by the next one?

Now think up a situation of your own. Make it something you are familiar with or at least think you are familiar with. On stage it is important to build from who you are and have been. Keep your performance simple. Think through the details. Don't worry about how you're going to come across to others; just concentrate on the physical actions that need to be performed, one by one. Try it out. Revise it. Try it again. Or throw it out and start over. Now try it in front of someone else. Get feedback and respond to it. Revise again. Present again. Once you are comfortable with your act, rehearse it, focusing more and more precisely on the smallest of details.

Another example: imagine that you're caught in traffic. You look at your watch and frown. A deep breath. You look around for something to occupy your attention. You start tapping your fingers on the steering wheel. What to do? You make faces to amuse yourself. Getting bolder, you start making faces at the driver in the next lane. Check the radio, run through the channels. No, you never *did* like that song. Nothing else but commercials. Another look at your watch. Damn. You hit the horn. Another deep breath. You slouch down, resigned to the wait.

What we are introducing here is a format that will structure these and future efforts. First, you'll be asked to call upon your own experiences. Once you are satisfied with your idea and what you have done with it, you'll share it with one other person. In this setting you'll give and receive specific and constructive feedback, modify your idea, and rehearse it. Then, you'll move to a group of four and repeat the process. Finally, from the group you'll nominate one or more acts for presentation to the entire class.

The value of this format is that by working in small groups where trust can be established, risk taking is encouraged; by focusing on constructive criticism and specific recommendations, a climate and process for change are established; by rehearsing your idea you'll really be able to fine-tune it; finally, by taking this amount of time and effort with just one idea, you will be able to polish it under controlled conditions. It is precisely this pattern we hope to encourage you to use once you reenter the day-to-day reality of your regular classroom. This kind of activity, by the way, may be a terrific tonic for teacher burnout.

Now that you've accomplished this much, try a duet instead of a solo. A partner can provide some security and license (you're not going it alone) as well as stimulation. Also, two characters allow for more dramatic possibilities.

As teachers, you'll need to consider the applications of pantomime to the classroom. Below are some typical situations; you can certainly come up with more.

1. It's a Monday morning in February, and you want to walk in displaying all the energy you had the very first day of school back in the fall.

2. Your students are struggling with a particular problem or concept that you are presenting. You don't want to give them the answer; you want to join them in discovering it. So you yourself adopt an appearance and behavior that signify confusion.

3. It's Friday after school, and you're tired. But one of your colleagues needs to talk. Take a deep breath (literally, figuratively, or both) and prepare for some active listening.

4. You're angry at the poor performance of a particular class on a recent test. They didn't take it seriously.

5. Join with your students in a deep belly laugh. (No sounds!)

6. It's the last day of school, and you're sad to see your students leave. They need to know that they'll be missed.

7. You're dissatisfied with the comments you received from your principal on an evaluation, and you are practicing looking assertive.

8. You're setting up a prank for one of your colleagues. Be mischievous.

9. It's another one of those damn meetings. Act immature.

10. More paperwork, more forms. Be hostile.

11. You're a new teacher, and it's the first day of class. You're overwhelmed.

12. You draw duty at the after-school social. An eighth grader asks for a dance. You bravely try a two-step.

13. It's a lesson on dinosaurs. Everyone, including you, has to become one.

14. Your salary raise has come through. You excitedly start figuring all that you will accomplish with it but quickly realize how little there actually is to go around.

15. A colleague gets singled out for praise by the principal. Be jealous.

chapter six

Voice

In a profession that is so dependent upon speech, it is amazing that so little is done to develop and train teachers' vocal capabilities. We are all left to adapt and adjust our teaching to the limitations we bring to the classroom. While we lavish energies on the content of our courses and on methodological growth and refinement, we ignore such presentation skills as projection and control of the voice. Teachers need to become more aware of its nature and its capacities; they need to distinguish the aspects of quality, pitch, volume, pace or tempo, and rhythm.

Listen carefully to the best and worst of teachers

Figure 8. Dr. Joe Weitz, professor of earth resources, has learned to relax with teaching, and now both he and his students are enjoying class more. He's made a distinct effort to talk less like a pedant and more like a normal person.

and notice the differences. Ineffective instructors usually have little vocal variety; their monotone is deadening. But that sameness is not limited to pitch alone. Poor teachers also bore with a sameness of volume— except when provoked to rage—and timing. Good instructors, whether or not they are conscious of it, typically have a well-developed vocal repertoire, and they use it. Of course, they are not undiscovered Oliviers—countless fine teachers have never "performed" in the narrow sense of the word—but they do understand the importance of variety in vocal expression.

They also know the value of the *absence* of sound. While ineffective teachers may end up shouting in an attempt to regain control of a class, the best teachers will often lower their voices to an ominous quiet to demonstrate concern. While poor instructors often become terrified by the slightest pause, connecting thoughts and utterances with "um's" and "ah's" and similar meanderings, good teachers are able to use silence quite effectively. An important thought dramatically delivered can be punctuated and extended by silence. In fact, one of the most important tasks of any teacher is to overcome this fear of silence. Students can be challenged really to think through an idea, but not if the teacher interprets every extended pause as either disinterest or lack of productive

Figure 9. Dorothy Guerin is a university counselor and adviser who works with students on improving their communications skills. The photograph is taken from a videotape of her final exercise in the Teaching as Performing workshop (playing the role of a student whose life is crowded with people and events but who can think of nothing to say). Our class has improved her teaching style. She learned to use well-timed pauses; she also learned that a class or workshop has to be rehearsed if it is to be successful. It won't just happen.

activity. Timing often differentiates the good from the bad teachers—the former conscious of the limitations of lecture and the value of timing, the latter seemingly oblivious to audience reaction, losing much of the import of their conclusions in some elongated monologue. Pauses are the punctuation marks of speech.

When we think about the kinds of regular training that vocalists undertake just to maintain their skills, let alone develop their potential more fully, we are reinforced in our conviction about the need for similar study and exercise by teachers. Although vocal capabilities are intimately linked with physical inheritance, vocal development is largely a matter of training, opportunity, and utilization. A diligent student can accomplish miracles with even the most modest of genetic endowments, while the very best abilities are often squandered by those of us who teach. Training and practice, then, develop the strength and flexibility of one's voice. These qualities in turn can infuse a lesson with intensity, variety, and drama. In teaching, the voice is a precious resource.

As we move to this particular aspect of the teaching art, we also have to reckon with the reasons why instructors do not naturally do more of what we suggest. As has been said before, there certainly is little if any attention paid to voice and vocal training within the confines of the traditional teacher preparation program. But an equally significant factor is one we keep coming back to: teachers' conservatism. The norm for teachers has long been one of "proper" decorum in their approach to instruction: a discrete public manner that can be a model for that next generation. As such, they are not given to risk and display but rather to carefully orchestrated master plans of scope and sequence—precisely what the students expect. What we are asking you to do is simply defy this normative tradition and come down much more heavily on the side of instruction—what gets kids to learn. You are really poorly trained as agents of socialization. Besides, it's much more fun to be occasionally outrageous.

Students at all levels consistently respond positively to an instructor's enthusiasm. And they seem to have special antennae that detect when a teacher would rather be somewhere else. No matter what the content of the course, there is an element of energy that seduces students of all ages. We've already discussed movement, which can be both cause and effect of an energetic attitude; what would this enthusiasm *sound* like? How do you capture it?

Vocally, energy can be understood by recalling those times when you were excited—when, say, you were provoked into speaking about something you consider extremely important. Your pitch rose, your volume increased, and your pace may have speeded up. Any time you enter a classroom, you should take a few moments and muster the energy to bolster your speaking. Students will pay more attention to dynamic speech, and you, in turn, will be reinforced accordingly.

EXERCISES

You have to promise that you'll try these. For those of you who have not studied voice or been involved with a choir or musical production, vocal warm-ups may seem weird—and they are, sometimes. But they are also critical for the development of your voice.

First come the general physical warm-ups. Unlike

Figure 10. Dr. John Lueck, associate professor of music, has worked with us in developing the voice component of our training. He's an experienced baritone himself.

other musical instruments, when it comes to voice you are your own instrument. The better your conditioning, the better potential for your instrument, your voice.

The warm-ups described in chapter 3, with some variations, would be a good place to start. Stretch and relax your body, from top to bottom, but focus special attention on your face, neck, and abdomen.

1. Rotate your neck and head.

2. Rotate your trunk from the waist.

3. Tighten and relax the different muscle groups: face, neck, shoulders, stomach.

4. Up on your toes and with hands above your head, stretch up; then swing your hands down as you bend your knees, then go back up on your toes.

5. With hands above your head, circle from the waist to the right and then to the left.

Now for your vocal equipment.

6. Wiggle and waggle your lower jaw. Many articulation problems stem from lazy jaws.

7. Give your tongue a good shaking.

8. Repeat the following sound combinations.
   brrrrrr
   ta ta ta ta ta
   me me me me me
   us us us us us
   la la la la la
   ha ha ha ha ha
   bee boy by beau boo
   dee day die doe do
   analogous combinations of consonants and vowels
   Now do these more quickly, then more slowly.

9. Go back to point 4 and add sound. Up on your toes, say "aahh" as high as you comfortably can, dropping your voice as you swing down and then raising it again as you come up.

10. Do the same with point 5 as you circle.

11. Work on breath control. Take an eye dropper, remove the rubber cap, and inhale and exhale

deeply and SLOWLY through the little tube. Take as much time as you can with the exhaling. Do this five times a day, every day. In a week or two, your lung capacity will have improved.

12. Work on "backing up" your words: have the energy and force come from the *diaphragm* rather than from the throat. Open up and relax the throat (the throat is most relaxed and open during and immediately after a yawn).

13. Bellow deeply, like a bear, to clear the throat. Feel your cords resonate; become more acquainted with the *range* of your voice (it's greater than you think).

14. Take an introduction to one of your classes (the start of the lesson) and "sing" it. Move around. Add gestures. Really ham it up and sing. This is a great way to break down any tendencies toward a monotone and to add some pizzazz to your lesson. It also gets you "psyched" and frees you from those morning blahs. (A word of caution: shut the door for this one. Some of your colleagues might not understand.)

15. Finally, take the risk and join a choir or audition for a play or musical. It will do you good, not only for development of skills but also for the excitement of performing that can then be translated back into your classroom.

chapter seven

Energy and Control

At the end of the last chapter, we were talking about the energy one needs to improve vocal performance. But the quality of energy—both how to call it forth and how to control it—is by no means limited to voice. Just about everything we do in class depends on the ability to reach back and find in ourselves the energy that will, for instance, transform a stale lesson into a fresh one, control an unruly bunch of kids, or illustrate general ideas with vivid movements of the body, hands, and face. On the other hand, there are those teachers who have to deal with the problem of too much energy in themselves. How can they channel

Figure 11. Performing techniques have helped Pamela Sachs primarily with her energy level. As a graduate student in counseling, she finds that without energy, she's unfocused and unable to take much in; with it, she can maintain a lightheartedness that keeps her classwork balanced and enjoyable. As a counselor, she finds it absolutely essential to be "on"; when she is, it's contagious. She sees herself as an encourager, a motivator, and a positive resource for students and other staff.

it into more effective teaching or tone it down so that it does not become the source of nervous distractions?

Before tackling specific questions like the above, keep in mind a few general directives. First, when preparing for a class, look for opportunities to be energetic. Add examples or issues that will animate you in class. Find controversial material. And do not be afraid to draw from your own experience to supply examples or illustrate a point. One teacher observes that whenever he talks about himself, the students perk up and pay more attention to what he is saying. They are always surprised (surprise, of course, can be a wonderful pedagogical tool) to find that the teacher is also a human being, with a past and a collection of experiences not totally unlike their own. Part of the success of this technique comes from the energy and expressiveness that inevitably enter your speech when you talk about yourself. This technique can certainly be abused, but when used sparingly it can be remarkably effective.

Second, prepare yourself by taking a few moments before each class and focusing on your objectives. That is precisely analogous to what an actor must do before embarking upon a particular scene: What do I need to *do?* What actions are necessary for getting what I want? he asks himself. The term "action," in many acting classes, refers to specific intentions and the physical movements associated with them. "What do you *want* in this scene?" the director asks the harried performer over and over again in rehearsal. If that performer does not have a concrete idea of what his character's intentions are, both explicit and implicit, the acting will often turn out to be vague and unconvincing. Similarly, the teacher must be just as sure about the particular intentions shaping a class.

Third, constantly elicit feedback on your progress and your successes. Regularly hand out student evaluations that include specific questions about your presentations, or invite colleagues in to observe and offer a critique, or tape some of your classes and *listen* to yourself (you will be amazed at what you are *not* aware of about the way you speak).

Finally, do not forget some of the basics; they may be truisms, but without an awareness of them teachers will have a far more difficult time. To be an effective teacher, you have to know your material and be prepared. You should enjoy being with kids. It really helps to be an optimist, considering how often teachers are made scapegoats, by the public and the media, for many of their students' problems. And a touch of the absurd goes a long way. (One professor of education routinely advises prospective teachers to cultivate an appearance of occasional insanity. Once established, such "strangeness" is in reality a convenient license for doing almost anything in the name

Figure 12. Social studies and Spanish teacher Paul Roper is basically a shy person; the performing class gave him the tools to be what he needed to be in order to teach effectively—to convey excitement or anger or just to emphasize a particular point. and at those times when he's not in the mood to teach at all, he will draw upon which he learned in our class to generate the necessary enthusiasm. Paul has also found himself using this technique with his son J.C.: after a long day of teaching, he will use our suggestions to call up the energy he wants to have for his demanding five-year-old son.

of what is right for kids and learning. Risk taking becomes much easier. The expectations of others may in fact become a prod for creative activities instead of a straitjacket.)

"But," you still ask, "how do I get that energy? When it's Monday morning and I barely got all the papers graded the night before after watching that television special, or it's Friday before the big game and I'm tired of hassling, or it's January and the cold and dark have created universal depression, or it's the same damn material I've taught time and time again, or it's that same damn kid or class that I'm just plain tired of—what do I do?"

How, in other words, do you get the energy you need day in and day out? And how do you control it? Well, consider two techniques commonly used by performers, each of which requires a few moments of preparation. There is nothing automatic in either of them, but both will enable you to achieve the appropriate level of energy, whether that be higher or lower than what you normally have.

EMOTIONAL RECALL

Ever since the visit of the Moscow Art Theater to this country in 1923, American actors, teachers, and critics have been debating the meanings and applicability of what Konstantin Stanislavski called "emotional memory" (also called "memory of emotion" and "affective memory"). Paying attention only to the paper theorists, one might conclude that there is little consensus; but talking to enough actors makes pretty clear what it is and how it works. To avoid confusion, we are using the term "emotional recall," which describes the same phenomenon. Robert Lewis, author, director, and teacher of acting, has explained concisely what is involved:

> The first thing to achieve in performing an Emotional Memory exercise is complete physical relaxation. In order for feelings to flow properly it is important to be muscularly free. First, it is advisable to sit in a comfortable position. Then, aided by your willpower, relax your muscles until all tensions disappear. Now start to concentrate on an incident chosen from your life that you feel will summon up an emotion similar to what is required in the scene. The incident should be one that made a real impression on you emotionally. Preferably, it should have taken place some time ago rather than recently. . . . Be careful you do not try to remember how you *felt* at that time. Rather, recall and recreate all the physical circumstances of the occasion. Remember all the details of the place where the event occurred, the time of day, how everything looked, who was there and how they appeared. The ability to recall and, more importantly, to reexperience the sensory impressions of the incident is of primary concern. Our sensory re-creations are closely related to the problem of conjuring up emotional memory. Now, in detail, go over in your mind exactly what transpired. If it is a properly chosen strong situation from your life, you should soon start to experience emotion resulting from the recall. You can then use this emotion as you step into the scene you are to play.[8]

This is a technique that can be used in different situations for different purposes. We are considering

---

[8]Robert Lewis, "Emotional Memory," *Tulane Drama Review* 6 (Summer 1962), p. 55. Reprinted by permission of *The Drama Review*.

it both as a stimulus for energies that will improve the dynamics of a teacher's presentation and as a means of controlling energy. To the puristic actor who objects that the circumstances of the classroom are going to prevent the concentration necessary for emotional memory, we answer that the teacher's recall need not be nearly as intense and comprehensive as the actor's. And to the objections of the skeptical instructor who suspects this will lead to exhibitionistic extremes, our response is that most practitioners of this method stress the necessity for rational control and well-defined limits.

Here is an example of the technique. An actress was having trouble with a scene in which she was supposed to be terrified. After all, how often in our adult lives are we in situations that evoke real terror? To prepare for the scene, then, she recalled her experience as a child when she saw her little brother being attacked by a German shepherd dog. She did *not* try consciously to re-create her feelings; instead, she focused on images of sensory details: the cool spring evening and, most of all, the sounds the dog had made. With those terrible sounds in her mind, she applied herself to the circumstances of the scene, and it worked beautifully. Remember that the process is based on imagining concrete sensory details associated with the experience (object, face, smell) and focusing on them. By concentrating on that small but essential part of the experience, you can more easily revivify the appropriate feelings and energy.

Think back to instances when you were very ex-cited and enthusiastic. Pick a particular one. Close your eyes. Relax. Put yourself back into that situation, concentrating on its sensory details. See yourself there. Listen to the way you talked: the pitch, the volume, the timing. Now be yourself at that time. Talk through some of what you said. Gradually, you should feel those same feelings rising up in you.

This is not a simple exercise. You must be able to relax, focus, concentrate completely on your past, and then let your current mood fade and the desired energies and feelings take over. Try it. Practice relaxing and focusing. Experiment with recalling different events until you have gotten better at it.

TECHNICAL ANALYSIS

A second technique commonly used by performers is to study carefully the specifics of the energy or the mood that they want. Again, think back to a time when you or someone else was especially enthusiastic. What did that energy *look* like? What were its physical manifestations? Whatever they were, imitate them, being as specific as possible. Technical analysis is more of an *external* approach, while emotional recall is *internal*.

One teacher, a beginner in dance, gives an example of technical analysis. His choreographer emphasized the act of standing and walking confidently and correctly: chin up, chest out, arms smoothly controlled, etc. There was little concern with actually *feeling* confident (emotional recall would be used for that), only with *looking* so. At the outset it seemed to the teacher that far too much time was being spent on this one exercise, only a small part of the performance that spring. But the choreographer persisted, and she was right. When opening night finally did arrive, the teacher-dancer felt quite confident and danced his part enthusiastically and successfully. He is sure that studying the "mechanics" of confidence led him toward it.

This is also not as simple a technique as it might initially appear to be. Time must be taken before school or class for preparation, and you will need others for feedback about your progress. What is especially exciting about this particular technique, though, is that if you make yourself appear to be energetic and perform the specifics of being enthusiastic, you will actually find yourself entering those states of mind. That may be the ultimate benefit: its renewing effect on you, the teacher.

chapter eight

Improvisation

When you begin to study the performing arts, you quickly realize the extent of the training and practice required. Admittedly, this can be discouraging, especially for teachers who merely want to enrich what they are doing in the classroom. While we cannot offer any quick and easy shortcuts, we can recommend improvisation as an intermediate activity that may augment expressiveness. Since improvisational activities are a crucial part of chapters nine and ten, we need to point out the benefits of the process.

In their helpful book, *Improvisation*, John Hodgson and Ernest Richards outline several aspects of the training and the potential benefits.[9] First, improvisation cultivates spontaneity; performers learn to respond honestly and openly to the unexpected. Second, the creative approach necessary for improvisation stimulates ingenuity and flexibility in problem solving. Third, improvisation enables performers to escape the limitations of their own backgrounds and to capture and better understand what is very different. Finally, improvisation hones sensory skills and builds confidence, since the performers are denied direction and rehearsal and are asked to rely on whatever internal or external data they can uncover at the moment.

Whether they know it or not, teachers are involved in improvisational activities all the time. Actors may never really need to become proficient at improvisation; after all, formal performance is a carefully crafted production that leaves little to chance. The teacher, on the other hand, is constantly being called upon to improvise, as one unexpected interruption after another interferes with the regular classroom process. Lessons may be carefully planned over both the short and long haul, yet almost daily adjustments are necessary as students and materials collide. The problems and needs of both students and teachers interact in a dizzying dynamic that requires the utmost in spontaneity and ingenuity. Moreover, because of the poorly defined nature of school objectives generally (whether they are to be vocational or liberal, basic or broad), educational programs do not stay the same, as advocates and researchers interact to

[9]John Hodgson and Ernest Richards, *Improvisation* (New York: Grove Press, 1979). Reproduced by permission of Grove Press, Inc.

push the pendulum of change back and forth. Teachers, of course, get caught in the middle of all this as change after change sweeps through the system.

Improvisational training involves a sequence of activities intended to achieve ultimately a desirable degree of spontaneity and ingenuity. As with all of the performing arts, warm-ups are a necessary first step. Then come activities to strengthen observational skills, permitting actors to know more effectively the surroundings that form a part of their performances. Concentration exercises are equally important if performers are to be able to sustain a characterization in unexpected circumstances. Finally, practice becomes vital if actors are to overcome their fears of the unknown and develop the self-confidence they need.

For teachers, this kind of training can be valuable. First, of course, come warm-ups; we have been stressing their value from the very beginning. Physical warm-ups prepare the instruments of the trade—body, voice, gestures, and expressions—for what is to come and provide the flexibility that teachers need for the variety and responsiveness so critical to the learning process. Mental warm-ups focus on the lesson at hand: what you hope to accomplish that day. Being relaxed but alert will permit you to make modifications in your plans as the need arises.

Second, observational skills are important if teachers are to be able to sense when something is not working and certain changes are in order. Signs of restlessness or confusion in students should be noticed, whether in body posture, voice, or behavior. Perhaps most important, teachers should discover, through observation of the students and their communities, what the prevailing interests and values are. A knowledge of these will in turn lead to improved prescriptions. This last concern is especially critical where there are differences in background, values, and abilities between the teacher and some of the students: the culturally different student, the linguistically different, the handicapped, the unmotivated, the poor, those with only one parent at home or no one at all because everyone is working. The mainstreaming and integration of diverse student populations into regular classrooms are putting significant pressures on the teacher. Observational skills become critical if a teacher is to learn what these students' needs, hopes, values, and interests are. And as the evidence grows about the profound effect that the environment has on student achievement,[10] observational skills become that much more essential if teachers are to be able to enter communities and make use in their own teaching of what they themselves see.

Improvisation also improves concentration. In the midst of an almost daily pattern of interruptions, setbacks, unanticipated successes, time pressures, grade considerations, personal problems, etc., teachers need to learn how to persevere and "stay on task." As more and more demands are made on the teacher to individualize instruction and to meet the needs of quite diverse students in the regular classroom, teachers will find that improving their abilities to concentrate will help immeasurably.

---

[10]The best-known research study attesting to the powerful role of the environment on student achievement is the so-called Coleman Report: J. S. Coleman et al., *Equality of Educational Opportunity* (Washington, D.C.: U.S. Government Printing Office, 1966). Christopher Jencks, in *Inequality: A Reassessment of the Effect of Family and Schooling in America* (New York: Basic Books, 1972), reanalyzed the Coleman data and reached the same basic conclusion.

Finally, do not be put off by the difficulties of improvisations. They can be noisy, threatening to shy participants, and prone to disintegration. Their lack of structure takes some getting used to (the presence of some kind of guiding group leader is especially important). They can be very demanding. Inhibitions about "public displays" or "making a scene" must be discarded; you must learn to respond openly and honestly to the assigned task.

As you become more comfortable with the process, you will quickly see the payoffs in your teaching: new freedoms and choices that will make it more responsive and effective.

EXERCISES

1. Observe, take notes about, and discuss each of the following.
   a. Your students: their dress, manners, habits, carriage; their speech patterns, vocabulary, and slang; their interactions with you, with each other, with other teachers, with their parents; their study skills (or lack thereof); their classroom behaviors; their abilities and disabilities or special needs; their values and attitudes as reflected in all of the above.
   b. Your colleagues: what is it about them that you can pick up through careful observation that would help explain their behavior or thinking?
   c. Similarly, your building administrators.
   d. Yourself: how consistent are your values and beliefs with the way you behave?

e. The parents of your students: what can you learn from a more careful study that would give you additional clues about their children and how best to work with them?

f. The community where you teach: housing, population density, residential patterns with respect to ethnicity and social class; transportation; parks, recreation, and children's play, formal and informal; festivals and celebrations; churches and religious worship; architecture and maintenance; stores and shopping; values and attitudes as reflected in all of the above.

g. The school: maintenance; attractiveness; utility; lighting, heating, and cooling; organization; values and attitudes as reflected in all of the above.

h. Your own classroom: organization; attractiveness; evidence of student work or influence; lighting and temperature control; flexibility; values and attitudes as reflected in all of the above.

2. Practice concentrating through each of the following improvisations. Discuss your thoughts and feelings at the conclusion of each. If no group opportunity is available, try some of these by yourself. Or just think about how you would go about performing them.

a. Maintain enthusiasm with a class that is bored and unmotivated.

b. Maintain respect for a student who is disrespectful toward you.

c. Sustain your anger for a class that will not take your material seriously.

    d. Maintain high expectations for a group convinced that they are failures.

    e. For students who have misbehaved, insist that they accept the consequences. They knew the rules, and by misbehaving they accepted responsibility for the consequences.

    f. Insist that parents accept some of the responsibility for assisting your efforts at controlling behavior in the classroom.

    g. Insist that your building administrator take responsibility for a particular student. You have exhausted all options, and the disruptions continue. Your administrator wants you to stay with it longer.

3. Improvise the following scenes. Follow each with a discussion of your thoughts and feelings.

    a. One person is the teacher. All others are students who have some kind of handicap (use blindfolds, ear plugs, bandages to incapacitate limbs, etc.). Plan some kind of activity that involves most of the students. (This is an excellent exercise in human relations; it directly addresses issues and feelings related to PL 94-142, the "mainstreaming" law.)

    b. Divide the class in half according to some physical dimension (height, eye color, gender, age, clothes, shoes, etc.). Have each group come up with its own set of rules and norms that govern that subculture. Exchange members in small groups until all have had a chance to visit the other subculture at least once. This is a competition in which each group tries to discover the rules and norms that govern the other. Through it, people can make some discoveries about the pluralistic reality of many classrooms.

c. Set up debates on topical issues. Halfway through, have the participants switch sides.

chapter nine

Scenes
for Practice

Now comes the time to work more with actual performance. With the scenarios that follow, you will be able to put into practice what has been said about warm-ups, focusing, energy and its controls, and the various component skills of body, gesture, and voice. The first set of scenes contains suggestions for improvisation; the second, actual scripts to act out. Each of the scenes should apply to most levels of teaching, but if a particular scene does not fit your circumstances, adapt it.

The scenes are useful not just for those in a workshop situation, who are of course collaborating with others. They can also be valuable exercises for individuals who at *some* point will be able to test them in a class or with colleagues.

We have outlined a format for groups on preparing each scene:

1. Read the scenario and adapt it, if necessary, to your professional situation.

2. Decide exactly what it is you want to do. What are your specific objectives?

3. Analyze into component parts that which you want to work on: bodily movement and posture, gestures, facial expressions, voice, timing, as well as the content of your message.

4. Make notes to yourself for rehearsal.

5. With *one* other person, describe your approach, focusing in particular on what might be different from what you would normally do in that situation. Remember that change is a slow and painstaking process. If you are to be successful, "start small" and be specific with the changes you have in mind.

6. When you are ready to start, warm up and focus. Prepare yourself physically and mentally for what you want to do. Relax. Concentrate.

7. In turn, run through your performance and offer critiques of each other's work. Take notes. Be specific about what did and did not work for you and for your partner. Be constructive in suggesting improvements, and be open to suggestions. Take risks now in this safe, supportive environment.

8. Become a foursome with another pair. Briefly discuss your specific objectives, and then repeat your performance. Take notes on the feedback.

9. One volunteer from each group of four will be invited to repeat his or her performance in front of the entire class.

10. Summarize your final reactions to your own performance and progress. Make any necessary notes to yourself about additional practice that you might need and what you would be willing to try in your next class.

SCENE ONE

It is the first day of class, when many of the students' impressions are formed and fixed. You want to establish the right mood: excitement about the material and the semester or year ahead; pleasure over the prospect of working with these particular students; and confidence that it will be a productive time. Work on striking the right balance between control and informality. Without trying too hard to be likable, show that you care about the students and know more about their states of mind than they assume.

Adaptations (particular grade or class, subject matter, etc.)

Specific objectives

Components:
body

gestures

facial expressions

voice

rhythm

SCENE TWO

As you know, administrators typically get recognized only when there's a problem. Think of someone you work for. Greet him or her warmly. Express your feelings about the past year and the role that particular administrator played. Briefly discuss your hopes for the new year: how you might help and what help you would need. Do *not* consider this practice in "buttering up"; you may need to express some negative responses to the previous year, so that the *present* year will be better.

Adaptations

Specific objectives

Components:
  body

  gestures

  facial expressions

  voice

  rhythm

SCENE THREE

More and more evidence indicates the importance of students' staying on task (that is, sustaining their attention on the materials or skills to be learned, without taking too many breaks) in order to avoid wasting time.[11] As a teacher, you will need to be prepared and organized, have high expectations, and make effective use of class time. You should also individualize instruction: adjust your style and your demands according to the needs and abilities of the person or group you are dealing with. One group might respond best to some easy coaxing, another to more rigorous pressure. With these two ideas in mind—staying on task and individualizing instruction—prepare and deliver the same lecture to two contrasting classes, one class much quicker than the other.

Adaptations

Specific objectives

---

[11]Students' achievement has been strongly linked to the amount of time their teachers can keep them "on task." See W. J. Tikernoff, D. C. Berliner, and R. C. Rist, *An Ethnographic Study of the Forty Classrooms of the Beginning Teacher: Evaluation Study Known Sample,* Technical Report No. 75-10-5 (San Francisco: Far West Laboratory for Educational Research and Development, 1975). For a more general discussion of this issue, see D. C. Berliner's chapter, "Tempus Educare," in P. L. Peterson and H. J. Walberg, eds., *Research on Teaching: Concepts, Findings and Implications* (Berkeley, Calif.: McCutchan Publishing Corp., 1979), pp. 120–35.

Components:
body

gestures

facial expressions

voice

rhythm

SCENE FOUR

It is the next class after an exam, and you want to express disappointment over your students' performance. Now is the time for a little intimidation and a little guilt-stirring. Convince the students that doing poorly on a test is a more significant kind of failure than they have rationalized. Make them see that they have hurt themselves, not you. Invent particular circumstances (what subject, what kind of test, how badly they did) to guide the improvisation. Without these particulars, you may flounder.

Adaptations

Specific objectives

Components:
  body

  gestures

  facial expressions

voice

rhythm

SCENE FIVE

You hear a colleague making some derogatory comment about a student. Confront the colleague about this without alienating him or her. Play the diplomat.

Adaptations

Specific objectives

Components:
body

gestures

facial expressions

voice

rhythm

SCENE SIX

You have become frustrated with a few students who
are not paying attention in class. Confront them. First
do this during the class. Then vary the situation by
calling them aside after class.

Adaptations

Specific objectives

Components:
  body

  gestures

  facial expressions

  voice

  rhythm

SCENE SEVEN

Your students are having an especially difficult time with a particular concept or technique. Without being sarcastic, you want to show empathy. Be confused as you work through a particular problem with them. Discover the answer as part of the group.

Let them know that you are not infallible and that a certain amount of confusion is often natural and even necessary. Students are genuinely encouraged when they realize that the answers do not always come automatically and that even the "expert" can be stumped.

Adaptations

Specific objectives

Components:
body

gestures

facial expressions

voice

rhythm

SCENE EIGHT

Improvise a solo scene based on an important event or moment taken from the field you are teaching: for instance, Galileo's first use, late at night with everyone else asleep, of his astronomical telescope. Devise the scenes so that props and costumes are not important.

Adaptations

Specific objectives

Components:
  body

  gestures

  facial expressions

  voice

  rhythm

SCENE NINE

Come up with a scenario of your own.

Adaptations

Specific objectives

Components:
body

gestures

facial expressions

voice

rhythm

The following entries are actual mini-scripts instead of improvisational suggestions. Contemplate general intentions and specific objectives; decide whether emotional recall or technical analysis, or both, are appropriate; and memorize the lines along with a partner. Think also about movement and the right physical gestures.

SCRIPT ONE—FRIENDS

(*Somewhere outside of school, over coffee or a drink, two friends talk. X is approaching total "teacher burnout"; Y is not quite as disillusioned.*)

X: You know, with all the hours we put in, we should get time and a half—no, make that double time.

Y: Yeah, but the public would never see it that way. They think we're overpaid as it is. Raising the salaries of sanitation engineers is *one* thing—but *teachers* getting a pay hike? That's not the American way! That old saying is true: you get what you pay for.

X: But would it be that much different if the pay were that much better? Really different?

Y: (*Pause*) I don't know. I suppose it would. You'd probably get a brighter, more aggressive teacher who'd damn well press for even bigger changes. But no—no one wants that. We're here basically to socialize the little buggers, make 'em able to sit for hours on end at tasks which they have little use for. Discipline. Control. *That's* the game.

X: Which must be why it's so tough in the inner city. Where's the payoff for all that discipline? Twelve years of doing your homework and then *still* no job. And those kids have fewer role models to look up to. Teachers are nowhere to them.

Y: That does seem to be the picture.

X: God, the hours and the *hassles* . . .

Y: Hey, there are *some* benefits.

X: Name half of one, please.

Y: (*Laughs*) Cheap government milk.

X: Right, and it's probably that PCB-contaminated stuff from Michigan. It turns teachers into creatures from the black lagoon. I feel my gills growing.

Y: All right, I'll name you some benefits. One, teaching is working with people. I know that sounds trite, but I'd rather be dealing with human beings than with computers. Two, it's environmentally clean. Three, you *can* make a difference. Four, there's the challenge of orchestrating a whole class of kids through a controversial or demanding concept, handling each class a bit differently. I like that. And there's the need to stay young, to keep in tune—hell, to stay in shape to maintain the kind of pace you need. There's also lots of time off for projects like recuperation.

X: So why are we complaining?

Y: (*In a whispering, mock-confidential tone*) There's room for improvement.

SCRIPT TWO—YOUNG TEACHER

(*The setting is an empty classroom. A young teacher alternately paces across the front of the room, stands and stares out the window, and sits and reviews introductory materials and requirements for the first day. This is a good opportunity for a little pantomime on nervousness. Physically, what do you do when you get nervous? After a deep breath, the teacher stands by the desk and muses aloud.*)

T: Well, it's about to begin. Let me review again what I'll need to do. First, I should avoid wetting my pants. Go over names and addresses. Then me. The class objectives. My expectations. Have to set the right tone—serious, businesslike, but clear and enthusiastic. That's what the research says. HAH! What do they know? (*Starts pacing*) Sitting up there in those towers, divorced from the real world, what do they really know about the crap we go through out here, the dull routine, the bureaucratic hassles, the pushy parents, the inertia that prevents change . . . ? (*Getting worked up*) But worst of all, the kids, the brats, the brown-noses, the thugs, the great unwashed and unmotivated masses . . . (*Pause*) Damn, is it that bad? (*Pause*) No. You'll get into it when the bell rings and you can actually get started. (*Pacing again; pauses at the window, stares*) Where did the summer go? I had such great plans. Maybe that's why I'm tired: too many plans, too little accomplished. But I *was* ready, excited to get to work. (*Turns to empty class*) Will they like me? Should I care about that? What if I get too many jerks? (*Bell rings*) Damn. Here we go. (*Puts on a big grin*) It's show time. (*Imaginary students begin to file in*) Hi there. Hello. Hi. How are you?

SCRIPT THREE—DAY OF RECKONING

(*It's the middle of the year. Many of your students seem to be slacking off. The weather is cold, Christmas is gone, and spring is a long time away. Be businesslike.*)

T: O.K., time for some straightening out. Too many of you are really slacking off, and I'm not sure what to do about it. (*Pause, pace, stop*) I know it's not the most exciting time of year. It's cold and it gets dark too early and you've been at it for six months now and spring seems to be about nine light-years away. It's tough on all of us. It would be easy to give in to the blahs, to quit trying and just try to keep occupied with busy-work. (*Quietly and a bit menacingly*) But we're not going to do that, because I don't like to have my time wasted. Wasting time is lousy. (*Suddenly very loud and animated*) We are going to pretend that this is September again—hurrah, hurrah—and you have all that energy *back*. (*Clap hands or do something noisy*) Maybe you'll surprise yourselves.

SCRIPT FOUR—HELP!

(*The office of the department head (H). It's the end of the day, but the teacher (T) comes in quickly, with a sense of urgency.*)

T: I've had it.
H: (*Startled*) Take it easy. Sit down.
T: I need your help.

H: Fine. What's wrong?

T: I'm losing my students, and I've run out of ideas. I've tried everything. I'm starting to hate walking into that room.

H: What do you want me to do about it?

T: Come in and observe. I know you have lots of ideas, and the students speak well of you.

H: (*Checks calendar*) Well, how about . . . two weeks from Thursday?

T: No, I think I need you sooner. Like tomorrow.

H: Tomorrow? Why so soon?

T: I'm desperate. O.K.?

H: It can't be that bad.

T: It is. Tomorrow, before lunch?

H: I'm not sure. There's a lot I need to—

T: (*Interrupts*) Tomorrow. Come on.

(*Improvise the conclusion according to how convincing the teacher has been.*)

SCRIPT FIVE—CONFRONTATION

(*The end of the day. The teacher* (T) *is tired and would really like to get home, but he or she has asked a new student* (S) *to come by and talk. The student has done little work and needs a change in attitude.*)

T: Hi there.

S: Hello.

(*Pause*)

T: (*Struggling for an opening*) Do you know why I asked you to come by?

S: Not really.

T: Guess. (*No response*) You have no idea? (*Still no response*) All right, I'll suggest the obvious. You're not doing much work, and what you *have* done is pretty sloppy. What's the problem?

S: (*Pause*) I don't know.

T: Come on, loosen up. This meeting is not being graded.

S: What do you want? I'm trying in class.

T: Not nearly enough, then.

S: You expect too much.

T: No, I don't think that's true. I just expect what I think you're capable of. Listen, it's your life. But I don't enjoy watching you treat it so shabbily. How about it?

S: What do you want me to say?

T: (*Discouraged*) I don't know. I want you to get on with your work. You're bright; you've got potential. Don't waste it.

S: Fine. Can I go now?

T: I didn't know I was holding you against your will.

S: (*Leaving*) See you later.

T: (*Alone*) Rats.

chapter ten

How to Keep
It Going

We are not suggesting that a good teacher must also be a flashy showman. Do not think that a resonant voice and a flair for the dramatic are all one needs to be successful (remember the infamous Dr. Fox lecture; see page 2). We do maintain, though, that working at certain performing skills, including control and understanding of the body, face, and voice, can lead to better teaching. One does not have to be a stand-up comic to know something about controlling an audience and to use that knowledge in the classroom. One does not have to be a stunt man to learn about the body and its effects on observers. And one does not, of course, have to be a diva to appreciate the importance of vocal technique. The study and practice of performing skills can, among other things, help teachers improve their lecture style, make discussions more effective, hold the attention of students longer, deal better with unexpected or stressful situations, and enlarge the teachers' store of specific techniques.

There are many teachers who still must overcome the old prejudice that they are somehow cheapening their craft by looking at it from the performer's perspective. Their skepticism, however, is understandable. It is dangerously easy to abuse this approach so that it becomes little more than an egotistical flight into the worst kinds of dilettantism. ("Instead of *talking* about Hamlet and the gravediggers, class, I'll just read the scene out loud." . . . "Instead of explaining Newton, I'll *be* him.") But as long as we remain diligently aware of the possible and sometimes tempting abuses, we can usually avoid them. Let us study the world of performance—*not* because we're all frustrated actors, but rather because, as teachers, we are (whether we like it or not) part of that world.

We need to consider the problem of "how to keep it going": once started in the study of teaching as performing, how do you continue the progress on your own, after the workshop is over or even without the benefit of a workshop at all? How do you structure your environment so you can continue to take risks and develop your skills further? Who is available to provide the necessary support, direction, and feedback?

Figure 13. Marietta Rudolph gained a great deal from our training. An elementary reading teacher, she has improved her presentational skills. She has also developed a greater understanding of performing and its relationships to teaching. Now she finds that she's more confident and relaxed when she has to make presentations to peers or parents. Our work on gestures has helped her become more aware of what she does or does not do. She uses pantomime and dramatics with her students both to relax and to animate them. But perhaps most important, she tells us that the crazy things we did in class were helpful in stimulating even modest changes in her classroom behavior; now she does more demonstrations in class, and the response of her students has been positive.

FIND A SUPPORT GROUP

Consider first the idea of some kind of support group. If you have participated in a workshop based on this text, then your classmates become a valuable source of support. Because of what all of you have already gone through, there are both the bonds of shared experiences and the potential for trust and relaxed communication. If you were not part of a workshop, you can still find people who will serve the same purpose. Colleagues to whom you are close, a faculty member from a nearby school, your principal or department head, students (more about them in a minute)—there is a wealth of potential in these individuals, who are available and often eager to provide assistance if you ask for it.

Because of our emphasis on a nonthreatening environment that will encourage risk taking, we suggest that you look first to colleagues whom you trust. Share your ideas with them; invite them in to give you feedback. This will not only be useful to you, but also may interest some of your peers in the process and thus develop a new working group.

If a nonthreatening environment is so important, what role can administrators and students play? After all (you may be thinking), administrators are so involved with job- and salary-related evaluations, and students have no formal training in instruction or evaluation. Well, it is indeed a new relationship we are asking you to form with both groups. But don't misunderstand. This relationship may only work with some administrators or students; with others, you may not feel comfortable taking substantial risks. Still, don't sell them short; some of our communicative and organizational tensions in schools come in part from our underestimation of both groups.

There has been, for instance, a great deal written in recent years about the need for principals to be instructional leaders in their buildings. Yet we also hear about the heavy demands put upon their time and energies just to manage operations. Much of the stress related to administration, in fact, may stem from just this kind of frustrating conflict. If you are an instructor, though, go ahead and make a request for one of your superiors to attend a specific number of your classes and give you structured feedback. You may get some excellent assistance as well as contribute to meeting that administrator's desire to be an instructional leader. But *avoid* having him or her drop in on just one class; if that happens, the risks become too high and the situation too artificial.

Students are another generally overlooked resource for teachers. While perceiving administrators as superiors and adversaries may or may not get in the way of their being much help to you, considering students as inferiors will definitely close doors. Through their role as consumers, students (like infants who typically understand much more than they are able to verbalize) as a rule have a substantial understanding of the instructional process. At Colorado State University, we have developed a program wherein students are trained in the rudiments of pedagogy and then paired with a faculty member to provide structured feedback over a period of several weeks. The results have been encouraging: we have been able to document significant faculty improvements, and we can also demonstrate positive changes in students' attitudes about the realities of teaching.

OBSERVE THE
PERFORMING ARTS

A second strategy for keeping your progress going is to become a more serious, more observant spectator of the performing arts. Accept the assumption that you are a member of the performance guild, and take a professional interest in what your "colleagues" are doing. Many of us spend a good deal of time watching plays, movies, and television shows, even listening to the radio, without making any connection between what we see and hear and what we do on the job; yet there is much of value to be learned. Not only can we read about the kinds of training artists must undergo in each area (music, dance, theater), but we can also see them in action.

Enjoying a play or film and using it to learn or refine some skills, by the way, are by no means mutually exclusive activities.[12] In fact, the more one understands about, say, the actor's craft, the more pleasure there will be in watching a successful performance. And you don't have to be an expert or a published critic to be a discriminating viewer capable of valid perceptions about effective and ineffective acting. By trying to articulate what makes for a good or bad performance, you will discover standards and techniques that may guide your own actions in the classroom.

Become more critical (that term, the dictionary reminds us, "may imply an effort to see a thing clearly

---

[12]We are aware that there are crucial differences between the crafts of acting on the stage and acting in front of cameras. But for our purposes, we need not get caught up in discussing the distinctions; that belongs in acting class, not here.

and truly in order to judge it fairly"). Use your imagination in coming up with material to be analyzed. Take television news, for instance: not necessarily a performing art, but still useful. What are the chief characteristics of Dan Rather's delivery? (Most any national newscaster will do.) How does his style differ from, say, John Chancellor's? Notice the emphasis a newscaster places on particular words, on the modulations of the voice as it rolls through a sentence or a whole news item, or how different attitudes (dismay, skepticism, admiration, wonder) are conveyed by changing the expressions of voice and face. Or focus on local news programs. Why do so many anchorpersons sound the same? What is the model that they are all trying to follow? Try imitation; try parody (not at all the same thing). Remember that passive observation will not be enough: you can't expect to improve your own presentation just by watching others. But *active* observation, which involves thinking about what you have seen and asking questions and testing your answers by going back to see more, will almost inevitably lead to a more sophisticated awareness of possibilities and devices that can become part of your own resources. No, you will not start sounding like a poor copy of Rather—but you will know more about speaking effectively.

If you want to learn something about the value of pauses and silence, tune your radio to that strange, syndicated American prophet of the airways, Paul Harvey, and listen to the way he punctuates his sentences and structures whole news reports with the pregnant pause. Continue your lessons in timing by watching, with *both* eyes open, the monologue of a good stand-up comic. Focus more on the manner in which he tells a joke and the various responses he has to situations like a failed joke or an unruly audience. Again, we are *not* implying that your role as a teacher is necessarily analogous to someone like Johnny Carson's role as an entertainer; all we are saying is that there are skills, although in different contexts and with different aims, that are appropriate for *both* roles.

Films and plays probably offer the most opportunities for learning about performing skills. If you feel that you are floundering—that you just do not know enough even to begin looking critically at what is happening on the screen or the stage—turn to some of the written reviews. Film critics like Pauline Kael (*The New Yorker* magazine) or Richard Schickel (*Time*) and drama critics such as Kenneth Tynan or Walter Kerr often have interesting and instructive things to say about acting and actors. (Those are just a few of the best-known names, but you can usually find some local critics of merit. Some major cities are lucky enough to have exceptionally good critics.)

Be careful, though, about how you go about using these reviews; don't let them stifle your own perceptions. Even good criticism about acting is often disturbingly subjective, so you should not be discouraged over disagreements. Just try to understand *why* you disagree. The better reviews can be valuable not because they offer the Final Word, but rather because they are usually based on a considerable knowledge of film and drama, and they provide models for how to talk intelligently about a particular performance. And do not ever be conned by the narrow and confused assertion that "it's all just personal opinion, anyway." Reviewing may be a maddeningly uncertain discipline, but it is still based on the precious idea that it is not only possible but *important* to try to distinguish between the objective qualities of good, better, and bad.

See a film or play more than once. With any interesting performance, you will be surprised to discover how much you did *not* notice the first time around, when you were more caught up with plot and keeping the characters straight. Keep in mind what the critics whom you respect have said, and test that against what you yourself experience. Recall your emotional and intellectual responses when you first saw it, and be prepared to find out why and how those responses were provoked. If this sounds a bit too analytical, just remember that you are now approaching the show from a different perspective and with a different motivation. The actors and actresses up there are using their voices, faces, and bodies to communicate with an audience and to affect that audience in certain ways. Teachers are also "up there" to communicate with an audience and to affect that audience in certain ways. Perhaps we can learn a few things from these people who need to take performing skills so much more seriously than most of us do.

The discussion so far has been quite general. What follows is a list of concrete examples or "rules"; some illustrate what has already been said, while others point in new directions or merely serve to show how it is possible for a nonprofessional to think and write about acting in order to better understand and make use of it. We are still talking about how to become a more serious, more observant spectator of the performing arts, specifically acting. (Of course, the same kind of list can be made with music or dance. We are pursuing acting because we believe it has more direct connections with teaching.)

1. Try to be more aware of how actors use both voice and body. One teacher recalls an Atlanta actor's performance as Willy Loman in Arthur Miller's *Death of a Salesman*. What made it memorable? For one thing, it was so *clear*: the actor was always audible, even when his voice was low and muffled with pain. That comes about through proper use of the lungs and diaphragm: using them to support the words, rather than relying only on the throat and its muscles. Also, his body was always in harmony with Willy's state of mind. As the play took its course, his posture became more and more broken; he actually seemed to be a littler man by the end (the teacher didn't realize this until later, after thinking about the performance for a while). As teachers, the way we hold ourselves invariably says something about our attitude towards both ourselves and the group we are addressing.

2. In any kind of a group scene, watch the performers who are *not* the focus of attention. If they're good, they'll be just as believable in their passive, listening, peripheral state as they are when all eyes are on them: concentration is *always* maintained. Sometimes you'll notice an actor's eyes wandering when he's not speaking; sometimes the eyes will become set and unfocused. This often means a loss of concentration. He is merely waiting for his next cue, or perhaps he is checking out the audience. In any case, he is no longer living as the character. He is no longer really listening to the others and watching what is happening on stage.

The great Russian theoretician and teacher of acting, Konstantin Stanislavski, knew the importance of concentration. One of his main goals was to devise techniques whereby the actor could avoid the imposing distractions of an audience. Sonia Moore, one of his students and a great teacher in her own right, has written:

> Stanislavski saw that, probably because of the artificial atmosphere of the stage, in front of a mass of people an actor's senses are often prone to paralysis. The actor loses the feeling of real life and forgets how to do the simplest things that he does naturally and spontaneously in life. Stanislavski realized that an actor has to learn anew to see and not just to pretend to see, to hear and not just to pretend to listen, that he has to talk to his fellow actors and not just to read lines, that he has to think and feel.[13]

If we substitute "teacher" for "actor" in the above quotation, it remains surprisingly apt. The group of students out there can be a difficult audience, forcing us consciously or unconsciously into unproductive poses, making us forget much of what we know about effective communication. Many teachers have certainly on occasion found themselves only "pretend[ing] to listen" to a student's question or comment, too intent on their own plan or on the clock actually to hear what that student is saying. "Concentration on a specific thought and a concrete action helps the actor to relax," writes Sonia Moore;[14] a facility for continuous concentration is essential for both actor and teacher.

3. Understand what some of the common faults are, such as overacting and indicating. The former

[13]Sonia Moore, *The Stanislavski System,* rev. ed. (New York: The Viking Press, Inc., 1965), p. 12. Reprinted by permission of the author and the publisher.

[14]Ibid., p. 66.

term is difficult to define; indeed, acting as a whole is difficult to write about, being the most ephemeral of the arts. Musical notes on a page, for instance, are a remarkably faithful record of what we will hear, compared to the huge gap between bare script and final production. Still, when you become acutely aware of an actor's working very hard and very obviously to achieve certain effects (so hard that you feel exhausted rather than exhilarated); when an actor seems too intense and out of step with the rhythm and style of the rest of the production; when an actor draws attention only to himself rather than to the play or film as a whole—these are often signs of overacting a part.

"Indicating" means signaling or telegraphing certain feelings and states of mind to the audience through conventional gestures instead of working on specific actions that will lead a performer, naturally and honestly, to those feelings. For example, someone will "indicate" frustration by rolling the eyes upwards, then shaking the head and snorting with disbelief or raising the hands with a "Why me?" shrug. "I am frustrated!" the actor is indicating to the audience— "Get it?" But do people really do that when they're frustrated? Do you? Rather than "indicating" an emotion, insist many acting teachers, you must genuinely *experience* it; then the right gestures (or telling *lack* of gestures) will come. Charles Marowitz has a clear definition:

> Strictly speaking, an actor cannot play fear, joy, suspicion, love, hate, etc. He *can* "indicate" these emotions—that is, by using an appropriate sign-language, he can convey dramatic information to spectators suggesting these states. But when he does this, he is

forced to resort to clichés. To avoid clichés, to experience these feelings organically, he must perform actions which will naturally produce them [the feelings] and, because they are real for him, they will have a greater plausibility for an audience.[15]

4. Look for and register the unexpected. One of the actor's most challenging tasks is to avoid stereotypes without becoming too mannered or eccentric. If a young person is playing a much older character, see if anything new and compelling comes across: a gesture, say, that is both interesting and truthful ("Yes, an old person *would* glare and fuss just like that in that situation, although I've never seen it"). Some of the most memorable moments in plays or films come when the performer upsets our expectations about how a scene or an emotion should be played. Asking questions of yourself can lead to discoveries: How does *this* portrayal of an old, sick person differ from other portrayals I have seen?

5. Talk about what you have seen! Compare your responses with friends who have some interest in drama or movies. Try to push them, as you are trying to push yourself, past purely subjective and fuzzy evaluations. If there are disagreements, explore them. The more you do this, the more confident you will become in the value of your own judgment about performing and performers.

6. Make a list of your favorite performers and performances or the most memorable scenes from plays

---

[15]From *The Act of Being: Towards a Theory of Acting,* by Charles Marowitz (Taplinger, 1978). © 1978 by Charles Marowitz. Reprinted by permission.

and films you have seen, or both. Try to explain *why* you have made these particular choices; once again, we are talking about moving towards a more analytical understanding of what you have watched. Here are a few examples drawn from our own experience.

a. Vivien Leigh as Blanche DuBois in the 1951 film version of Tennessee Williams's *A Streetcar Named Desire,* directed by Elia Kazan. She communicates such a wide range of emotions, all of them convincing: nervousness, hope, nostalgia, desperation, affection, distrust, fear, rage, confusion. Her performance is rich in the sense that there are so many details to notice: the way she darts her eyes about, quickly and insecurely, when she begins to lose self-control; the way the expression in her eyes changes as she responds to different characters; the light, fluttering quality of her face and body, suggesting something like frailty, but not quite that because of an inner resolve. Blanche is the kind of character that is easy to overact: hysterical Southern belle at end of rope. Yet Leigh manages to avoid all the clichés and give a performance that, like any substantial work of art, reveals new shades and new meanings every time it is seen.

b. Peter Sellers in the 1964 film version of Stanley Kubrick's *Dr. Strangelove or: How I Learned to Stop Worrying and Love the Bomb.* Sellers plays three different characters, and each one is difficult to forget. There is, first of all, the resigned and startlingly bald President of the United States, who cannot quite believe the way in which his country is being led toward nuclear war. He seems a decent fellow in a tank full of sharks; he is competent, authoritative when necessary, and wonderfully ordinary, even down to that bland American accent. Then there is the stalwart British officer, Group Captain Mandrake: resourceful, intelligent, and thus the perfect foil for all the madness surrounding him. When General Jack D. Ripper quietly asks Mandrake if he has ever undergone torture, his response ("Well, as a matter of fact, Jack, yes, I have") is self-effacing, slightly embarrassed, and completely human. Finally, of course, there is Dr. Strangelove himself: a crazy caricature of the inhuman scientist, whose body is as bent out of shape as his mind. The phrase "tour de force" is a cliché, but we will leave it at that anyway, since words are not quite adequate to describe Sellers's accomplishment in this film.

   c. Jackie Gleason as the down-and-out boxing manager, Maish, in the 1962 film version of Rod Serling's *Requiem for a Heavyweight*, directed by Ralph Nelson. Yes, Jackie Gleason—long before his "Smokey" days. Having a character's name stick in your mind is often one sign of an unusually good performance, and Maish is still vivid for many people. Gleason does not play an admirable or even likable character—yet there is so much that is *believable* in his portrayal of a man who must betray his friends in order to save his skin that you come away from the film wondering if you would have behaved any differently. His eyes are those of someone staring at a life without value.

PARTICIPATE IN THE PERFORMING ARTS

A third strategy: become an actual student of the performing arts. Take classes (many regional professional theater companies offer different kinds of instruction, ranging from beginning acting and voice to improvisation and oral interpretation). Participate in a local amateur theater or dance group or choir. Audition for parts, no matter how small. Don't be intimidated; experience is often not necessary. Many of these groups are more interested in enthusiasm and commitment than in dazzling talent, which is rare in the amateur context anyway.

We cannot emphasize too much the importance of stretching yourself through these occasional classes and amateur activities. Working on a few dramatic scenes would be more enlightening than sitting and reading what others have to say about acting; the same goes for sweating through a few choral rehearsals, which would teach more about controlling and improving the voice. Such participation often forms a pleasing chain reaction: taking a class can lead to a part that otherwise you never would have considered trying for; working with one group can give you the experience that another group is looking for.

There are always going to be plays performed at colleges and community theaters, which usually welcome new blood (the same goes for many choral groups, as long as you can carry a tune). Check the local papers for information on tryouts. If you are not quite ready to take the plunge, consider volunteering some time for off-stage work: helping with set construction or being an assistant director or stage manager. Again, these jobs do not require extensive experience, and they are a good means of getting to know some people and realizing that you just may be ready for that audition. By the way, do not let unfamiliar terminology scare you off. You can be an excellent assistant director, for instance, without knowing anything about directing. What you do is attend rehearsals and be a good observer so that you can help the director with a hundred odds and ends. One of the benefits there is that you learn a lot about both directing and acting.

Auditions themselves need be no more difficult than walking into a new class; in fact, the two situations have much in common. For both, you are confronting people—often strangers—who will be judging you, and the first impression has to be effective. Both situations often call for a certain degree of bluff and bluster: presenting a little more confidence, perhaps, than that which you are actually feeling. In a compressed period of time, you have to convey a fairly accurate idea of who you are and what you have to offer. There's no reason to regard the audition as something beyond your ken. You have been auditioning, in a sense, for as long as you have been opening that door and seeing all those "Well, what's so special about *you*?" expressions.

Be prepared with one or two memorized pieces, although in many tryouts you won't need them but will be asked instead to read from the play itself. Don't be put off by the confusion or the waiting or the subjectiveness or unfairness of it all. In many cases, those in charge are just as uncomfortable as you are, and they may not be master tacticians either. Most important of all, do not get discouraged if you are not immediately successful. There are so many factors involved in deciding who gets a part, whether it be large or small, that have to do neither with your talent nor with how you did at a particular audition— factors like physical appropriateness, age, and temperament of the judging director.

When you get a part, make sure that you have an

extra reserve of patience for the upcoming rehearsals. Preparing a play for performance is never the smoothest of operations. People of starkly contrasting personalities are suddenly thrust into a collaborative venture, and the chemistry of this situation produces both the joys and the frustrations that are an integral part of theater. Often, one of the principal frustrations is squandered time. Five or ten or twenty people working toward the same goal are just not going to move as efficiently as when you alone are planning and managing a course. Our own experience has taught us to expect several stages of feelings as rehearsals progress: (1) pleasure over getting a part; (2) disappointment with the initial awkwardnesses and low energy; (3) excitement as you and others begin to discover more about the play and its parts; (4) what we call the "where can we go from here?" letdown: there seem to be no more breakthroughs possible, and runthroughs become set and mechanical; (5) the "necessary nadir": everything is going wrong, and the play seems far worse than it was a couple of weeks previous; and (6) coming together: the pressures of time and opening night finally crystallize some or all of the play's potential and performances, and you actually do it. Of course, by this time you have been too close to the play for too long to maintain any kind of perspective; instead of fretting over its quality, just enjoy the experience as much as possible. After all, you're not doing this for a living.

At the risk of sounding trite, we will stress that you should not allow lack of previous experience to prevent you from going ahead and involving yourself in some kind of performance. Lots of experience can engender bad habits as well as confidence; being new at all this, moreover, can sometimes be a downright advantage, giving you a freshness and interest that others lack. Also, you are not in this alone: your director is the boss, and it is his or her responsibility to help you every step of the way.

Regardless of your teaching style, performing in front of an audience can only help you to function in the classroom. Confidence, voice and body control, concentration, energy—all of these can be enhanced when you join local productions. You'll find yourself growing in new ways.

As far as classes in acting and singing and dancing are concerned, we have already suggested how accessible they are. You can study in association with a local company, or at a college with the right course offerings, or at a community arts center, or privately (*seek recommendations* from the other suggested resources). Classes are by no means necessary for the kind of participation we have been talking about, but they will put you in touch with many people of similar interests and provide information about productions in your community.

BECOME A STUDENT AGAIN

Returning to the role of student actually represents a fourth strategy for keeping one's progress going. If you are to remain sensitive to the needs and difficulties of your students, be one yourself. Enroll in a continuing education class; pursue an old hobby or start a new one. Ask to sit in on the classes of colleagues from different fields. Take a professional day of leave and visit classrooms in other buildings. Take classes with professors who have reputations as excellent teachers. Continually contrast your knowledge and teaching experience with your role as a student.

You will be surprised to discover how much you have forgotten or taken for granted about what students have to go through. It's one thing to be theoretically aware of the pressures and moments of inadequacy; it's quite another to experience them firsthand. Perhaps you will be more patient (and consequently more effective) with students who need some extra help with a concept or a method *after* you yourself have been in the position of falling behind the competence of the rest of the class. One professor vividly remembers a welding class he took several years ago. He had just finished his Ph.D. and wanted a "real," down-to-earth skill, so he enrolled in a local vocational-technical school and eagerly donned his blue-collar shirt. Ten weeks later he was totally humbled when his fellow students, many of them high-school dropouts, had far surpassed him, leaving him sweating whenever his instructor would come around to observe the college professor at work. Another teacher recalls his experience with the frustration that results when understanding a skill does not lead immediately to its correct execution. After having tried for an hour to learn how to drive a car with a manual transmission, he felt guilty about the times he had expected from his students too much too soon.

Kill two birds with one stone, then, by being a student of the performing arts.

With all of these strategies, you can become more adept at "reading" yourself; in other words, self-awareness will be easier and more fruitful. When you "read" yourself well, you recognize when your body is tense from stress or when you are really challenging yourself and taking a significant risk. Most important, learn how to reward yourself when you have taken that big step, no matter what the results. Become more comfortable with risk taking, and be your own best supporter.

READ

Finally, reading more about the performing arts (acting and theater in particular) will supplement all the strategies we have been talking about. As with the learning of any craft, reading alone cannot do the job, but it can stimulate or renew one's interest in performance skills. This is not the place for an exhaustive bibliography, which would take up hundreds of pages. Instead, what follows is a select, annotated list of works that we have found most helpful and accessible. Many are paperbacks (so indicated in the individual entries), most are in print, and a good number are available also in major libraries. There are six categories: basic reference works; acting; movement, pantomime, and voice; creative dramatics; periodicals; and other related works. The focus is on acting and the theater rather than on other performing arts (music and dance) because the former fields include those aspects of music and dance—voice, movement, etc.—that are most relevant to teaching. Asterisks mark works of special interest.

BASIC REFERENCE WORKS

Chicorel, Marietta, ed. *Chicorel Index to the Spoken Arts on Discs, Tapes and Cassettes.* New York: Chicorel Library, 1973.
———. *Chicorel Bibliography to the Performing Arts.* New

York: Chicorel Library, 1972. Including both books and periodicals, this volume covers the history and the practice of such topics as acting, costume, dance, motion pictures, opera, pantomime, puppet plays, and theater.

*Handel, Beatrice, ed. *The National Directory for the Performing Arts and Civic Centers,* 3rd ed. New York: John Wiley, 1978. A valuable book that provides all kinds of information about "permanent" (relatively stable) performing arts organizations in the United States, listed by state.

*———. *The National Directory for the Performing Arts/ Educational,* 3rd ed. New York: John Wiley, 1978. A companion volume that supplies information on "all major schools and institutions [mostly colleges and universities] that offer training in the performing arts." This book will help you find local organizations that offer classes.

McGraw-Hill Encyclopedia of World Drama. New York: McGraw-Hill, 1972.

The New York Times *Film Reviews.* A multivolume series (published by the *Times* and Arno Press) covering the years 1913–1978, with new volumes issued periodically.

The New York Times *Theater Reviews.* The years 1870–1970 are covered.

*Schoolcraft, Ralph Newman. *Performing Arts Books in Print.* New York: Drama Book Specialists, 1973. An excellent annotated bibliography divided into four major sections: (1) Books on theater and drama (includes the topic "Drama in the Classroom"); (2) Books on technical arts (includes "The Actor and His Craft"); (3) Books on motion pictures, television, and radio; and (4) the mass media and the popular arts. Keeping this important book up-to-date is the periodical *Annotated Bibliography of New Publications in the Performing Arts*, also edited by Schoolcraft. All the books listed in these works are available from the American mecca of theatrical publications, The Drama Book Shop, 150 West 52nd Street, New York, NY 10019.

Whalon, Marion K. *Performing Arts Research: A Guide to Information Sources.* Detroit: Gale Research, 1976. Includes the chapter "Sources for Reviews of Plays and Motion Pictures."

*Willis, John. *Theatre World.* New York: Crown Publishers, Inc., annual. *The* reference for American professional theatrical activity, it surveys the work of Broadway, off-Broadway, national touring companies, annual Shakespeare festivals, and professional resident companies in the U.S. Chock full of photographs.

ACTING

Boleslavsky, Richard. *Acting: The First Six Lessons.* New York: Theatre Arts Books, 1933. A brief and entertaining book, in the form of a dialogue between the acting teacher and the naive "young creature" who wants to be an actress. This was the first book in America to present some of the theories and techniques of the master Russian actor-director-teacher, Konstantin Stanislavski.

Blunt, Jerry. *The Composite Art of Acting.* New York: Macmillan, 1966.

Chekhov, Michael. *To the Actor: On the Technique of Acting.* New York: Harper & Row, Pub., 1953.

*Cole, Toby, and Helen Krich Chinoy, eds. *Actors on*

Acting: The Theories, Techniques, and Practices of the World's Great Actors, Told in Their Own Words. New York: Crown Publishers, Inc., 1970. Paperback. The standard volume in the field, it has just about everything the amateur would want: introductory essays; biographies; a bibliography with over one thousand entries through 1969; and a massive selection of writings, almost all by performers, organized according to nation and time period.

*Hagen, Uta, and Haskel Frankel. *Respect for Acting.* New York: Macmillan, 1973. A book with a big following (ten printings in the first seven years). It is a coherent and carefully written account of "the Method," which is the Americanized version of Stanislavski's teachings. Although different actors and teachers will explain Method acting differently, Hagen is one of its best interpreters.

Hayman, Ronald. *Techniques of Acting.* London: Methuen, 1969. Written on the other side of the Atlantic, this text does not limit itself to a Stanislavski-oriented approach.

Hodgson, John, and Ernest Richards. *Improvisation.* New York: Grove Press, 1979. Paperback. First published in England in 1966 and revised in 1974, the book makes great claims for the value of improvisation in theater, education, and life in general. It provides good background and lots of exercises.

Glenn, Stanley L. *The Complete Actor.* Boston: Allyn and Bacon, 1977. One of the more comprehensive acting textbooks, it covers Greek theater, Shakespearean tragedy, and comedy in addition to the fundamentals of training. Excellent and abundant exercises.

McGaw, Charles. *Acting Is Believing: A Basic Method for Beginners.* New York: Holt, Rinehart & Winston, 1966. A textbook used in many American schools, it is based on those aspects of Stanislavski's system that are helpful and accessible to the beginner.

MacKenzie, Frances. *The Amateur Actor.* New York: Theatre Arts Books, 1966.

Marowitz, Charles. *The Act of Being: Towards a Theory of Acting.* New York: Taplinger, 1978. A fascinating treatment of acting and related matters by an American-born man of the theater who has done much of his work in England. Besides giving his experimental exercises and iconoclastic views on the rehearsal process, Marowitz also provides a clear critique and summary of American Method acting in the chapters "Stanislavski and After" and "A Simplified Method."

*Moore, Sonia. *The Stanislavski System: The Professional Training of an Actor.* Penguin, 1976. Paperback. A simplified guide to the Russian's teachings, including explanations of such terms as the "magic *if,*" emotional memory, and super-objective. Should be read in conjunction with Moore's other work (see below).

*———. *Training an Actor: The Stanislavski System in Class,* rev. ed. Penguin, 1979. Paperback. Sonia Moore imitates the technique of her master by making points within the framework of actual classroom situations. The text is based on tape-recordings of her classes in New York City.

*Spolin, Viola. *Improvisation for the Theater: A Handbook of Teaching and Directing Techniques.* Evanston, Ill.: Northwestern University Press, 1963. A pioneering work based on a lifetime of teaching, experimenting, and inventive game playing, the book is by no means limited to the training of actors. It is closely related to the concerns of "teaching as performing."

*Stanislavski, Konstantin. *An Actor Prepares,* trans. by Elizabeth Reynolds Hapgood. New York: Theatre Arts Books, 1936. Although scholar and translator David Magarshack has pointed out that this edition is a substantial abridgment as well as a translation (see his introduction to *Stanislavski on the Art of the Stage* [London: Faber and Faber, 1967]), many actors still consider it the "Bible" of their craft. For them, it is the one book needful.

———. *Building a Character,* trans. by Elizabeth Reynolds Hapgood. New York: Theatre Arts Books, 1949. The sequel to *An Actor Prepares.*

MOVEMENT, PANTOMIME, VOICE

Anderson, Virgil A. *Training the Speaking Voice,* 2nd ed. Oxford University Press, 1961.

Christy, Van. *Expressive Singing,* 3rd ed., vols. I and II. Dubuque, Iowa: Wm. C. Brown, 1974–75.

Desfosses, Beatrice. *Your Voice and Your Speech: Self-training for Better Speaking,* rev. ed. New York: Hill & Wang, 1959.

Hamblin, Kay. *Mime: A Playbook of Silent Fantasy.* New York: Doubleday, 1978. Paperback.

Hunt, Douglas, and Kari Hunt. *Pantomime: The Silent Theatre.* New York: Atheneum, 1964.

King, Nancy. *Theatre Movement: The Actor and His Space.*

New York: Drama Book Specialists, 1971. Paperback.

Machlin, Evangeline. *Speech for the Stage,* rev. ed. New York: Theatre Arts Books, 1980.

Pisk, Litz. *The Actor and His Body.* New York: Theatre Arts Books, 1976. Paperback.

Rubin, Lucille, ed. *Movement for the Actor.* New York: Drama Book Specialists, 1979. Paperback.

Wall, Joan, and Ricky Weatherspoon. *Anyone Can Sing.* New York: Doubleday, 1978.

CREATIVE DRAMATICS

Creative dramatics is a teaching technique primarily for younger students, in which they perform scenes and improvisations. See "Drama in Education" in the card catalogue.

Complo, Sister Jannita Marie. *Dramakinetics in the Classroom.* Boston: Plays, Inc., 1974. Paperback.

Courtney, Richard. *Play, Drama, and Thought: The Intellectual Background to Drama in Education,* 3rd ed. New York: Drama Book Specialists, 1974.

Durland, F. C. *Creative Dramatics for Children: A Practical Manual for Teachers and Leaders.* Kent, Ohio: Kent State University Press, 1975. Paperback.

Fitzgerald, Burdette. *World Tales for Creative Dramatics and Storytelling.* Englewood Cliffs, N.J.: Prentice-Hall, 1962.

Heining, Ruth, and Lyda Stillwell. *Creative Dramatics for the Classroom Teacher.* Englewood Cliffs, N.J.: Prentice-Hall, 1974.

Hodgson, John. *The Uses of Drama: Acting as a Social and Educational Force.* New York: Grove Press, 1979.

McCaslin, Nellie. *Creative Dramatics in the Classroom.* New York: D. McKay, 1968.

Parry, Christopher. *English through Drama: A Way of Teaching.* Cambridge, England: Cambridge University Press, 1972.

Siks, Geraldine, and Hazel B. Dunnington, eds. *Children's Theatre and Creative Dramatics.* Seattle: University of Washington Press, 1967. Paperback.

Wagner, Betty Jane. *Dorothy Heathcote: Drama as a Learning Medium.* Washington, D.C.: National Education Association, 1976.

PERIODICALS

These are some of the more established journals that are found at many libraries.

American Film (American Film Institute)

The Drama Review (School of the Arts, New York University; from 1957 to 1967 this was the well-known *Tulane Drama Review*)

Film Comment (Film Society of Lincoln Center)

Film Quarterly (University of California Press)

Plays and Players (a London monthly that focuses mostly on the English theatrical scene)

Quarterly Journal of Speech (University of Missouri)

Sight and Sound (British Film Institute)

Theater (Yale School of Drama)

Theatre Critics' Review (compiles New York reviews in their entirety)

Theatre Journal (University and College Theatre Association)

OTHER RELATED WORKS

Billington, Michael, ed. *Performing Arts: A Guide to Practice and Appreciation.* New York: Facts on File, Inc., 1980.

Brook, Peter. *The Empty Space.* New York: Atheneum, 1969. Paperback.

Clurman, Harold. *On Directing.* New York: Collier Books, 1974. Paperback.

Davitz, Joel. *The Communication of Emotional Meaning.* New York: McGraw-Hill, 1964.

Goffman, Erving. *Strategic Interaction.* Philadelphia: University of Pennsylvania Press, 1970. This is a monograph in the University of Pennsylvania series "Conduct and Communication."

Greer, Peter, ed. *Why Pretend? A Conversation about the Performing Arts with Errol Hill.* San Francisco: Chandler and Sharpe, 1973.

Lowry, W. McNeil, ed. *The Performing Arts and American Society.* Englewood Cliffs, N.J.: Prentice-Hall, 1978.

Olfson, Lewy, ed. *Fifty Great Scenes for Student Actors.* New York: Bantam, 1970. Paperback.

Steffensen, James L., ed. *Great Scenes from the World Theatre.* New York: Avon, 1965. Paperback.

Tynan, Kenneth. *The Sound of Two Hands Clapping.* New York: Holt, Rinehart & Winston, 1976.

chapter eleven

Teachers in Literature

Over the years the authors have compiled a small repertoire of literary texts depicting various teaching situations seen through the eyes of poets, novelists, and playwrights. These texts can serve a number of purposes: form the basis for discussion about aspects of teaching and the student-teacher relationship; be the source for dramatic readings, which provide an opportunity to practice and polish one's presentational skills; lead to improvisations performed by teachers or student-teachers as a means of exploring the meanings of the text and its applications to their own work. What follows are a few of these excerpted texts, with comments that may stimulate more ideas and enrich the repertoire.

WALT WHITMAN, "WHEN I HEARD THE LEARN'D ASTRONOMER" (1865)

> When I heard the learn'd astronomer,
> When the proofs, the figures, were ranged in columns
>   before me,
> When I was shown the charts and diagrams, to add,
>   divide, and measure them,
> When I sitting heard the astronomer where he lectured
>   with much applause in the lecture-room,
> How soon unaccountable I became tired and sick,
> Till rising and gliding out I wander'd off by myself,
> In the mystical moist night air, and from time to time,
> Look'd up in perfect silence at the stars.

Think back to that biology professor we described in the introduction. His love for the material was just not enough for its successful communication. The manner and attitude of Whitman's erudite astronomer, although sanctioned by the crowd's polite applause, are in conflict with a more natural, intuitive approach to the subject. "The learn'd astronomer" creates a gap between his subject and our own curiosity about the meaning of it all. The speaker of the poem must leave the lecture hall and simply watch the night sky, alone, free to approach certain unspeakable meanings in the stars that cannot be easily dissected or conceptualized. We are not trying to reduce this fine poem to a lesson on teaching methods. Like any significant work of art, it suggests more than can be easily pinned down in a tired maxim. The poem is about, among other things, different ways of perceiving, knowing, and feeling about the immensity of the universe. Still, the poem does address the idea of lecture-hall dryness and formality, which create too big a gap between the experience of the classroom and the subject being "taught."

When reading the poem aloud, one should pay attention to its pauses (signaled by the commas) and the rhythm of the lines. Notice that the first four lines grow longer and longer as the poet becomes more and more bogged down in those "charts and diagrams." Relish the rich, hushed sound of "mystical moist night air": enunciate each word slowly so that we can hear all the corresponding consonants clotted together in "mystical" and "moist." And make sure to register the perfectly regular beat or meter of the last line (straight iambic pentameter: "Look'd úp in pérfect sílence át the stárs"), which contrasts with the preceding irregular lines and helps to create a mood of calm, balanced stillness.

Many useful and enjoyable improvisations can be derived from Whitman's poem (remember what we have said about the benefits of improvisation: see chapter eight). They can range from straightforward re-creations of the general situation to thoroughly unconventional dramatic events that somehow grow from or are inspired by the poem. All one needs is a group of people interested enough in teaching to flex their imaginations and take some risks. They may be able to benefit from this kind of interaction, which calls for many of the skills necessary for good teaching: mental and physical agility, confidence, the ability to stimulate human energies and deal with the unexpected, etc. Consider the following treatments of the poem.

1. *A* is the astronomer (or anatomist or zoologist or ...), *B* is the "tired and sick" auditor, and the rest are the approving multitude. At some point *B* will rise and leave to watch in silence some natural phenomenon related to *A*'s discipline. Postimprovisation discussion should focus on this gap between analysis and wonder.

2. Same scene, but this time *B* interrupts the proceedings and attempts to explain what is wrong. The audience reacts with decorous disapproval; *A*'s reaction is up to the player (condescending patience? barely concealed impatience? genuine concern? bewilderment?). Postimprovisation discussion should deal with the lecturer's feelings.

3. One player is the lecturing scientist, who cares very much about his presentation (the player must choose a discipline about which he can talk with knowledge and ease) and is making it in a conventional way. The rest are bored students or listeners who, for one reason or another, are not following it very closely. For a while they must pretend to listen; then, one after another, they begin to vocalize their thoughts ("I'd rather be outside ..."; "When is this going to end ... ?"; "I don't know or care about what he's saying ... ," etc.), still maintaining the physical postures of respectful attention. They should begin quite softly but grow progressively louder. The lecturer continues with his talk, for he of course does not "really" hear these mental divagations. Finally, at the point of chaos, he must change his style to do whatever is necessary to *stop* the noise and make the philistines genuinely interested in what he is discussing.

GARY GILDNER,
"FIRST PRACTICE" (1969)

Quite a different kind of lecture is the subject of Gary Gildner's ironic little poem, "First Practice."[16] Gildner presents us with a stock character whom most of us have encountered at some point in our lives as students: the fanatical athletic coach who cares only about winning and who, for that purpose, is intent on instilling in his young innocents the values of cunning and violence. You may want to supply quotation marks, although the poet omits them deliberately, for the disorienting effect. Also, to the impressionable young speaker, Mr. Hill is such a threatening presence that his words are too immediate and imposing to be set off by the mechanical decorum of inverted commas.

> After the doctor checked to see
> we weren't ruptured,
> the man with the short cigar took us
> under the grade school,
> where we went in case of attack
> or storm, and said
> he was Clifford Hill, he was
> a man who believed dogs
> ate dogs, he had once killed
> for his country, and if
> there were any girls present
> for them to leave now.
>   No one
> left. OK, he said, he said I take
> that to mean you are hungry
> men who hate to lose as much

[16]Reprinted from *First Practice* by Gary Gildner by permission of the University of Pittsburgh Press. Copyright © 1969 by University of Pittsburgh Press.

as I do. OK. Then
he made two lines of us
facing each other,
and across the way, he said,
is the man you hate most
in the world,
and if we are to win
that title I want to see how.
But I don't want to see
any marks when you're dressed,
he said. He said, *Now*.

Here we have an instructional process that is powerful yet repulsive, rigorous yet dehumanizing. Some would call it exploitative. Mr. Hill's is a style often emulated on the playing fields (shades of Lombardi) but unacceptable in the classroom.

This poem, by the way, works well in poetry-class discussions because it is accessible, it appeals to the common experience of students, and it reads well in its play with language and form. This last quality makes itself clear when the poem is read aloud and emphasis is placed both on the way in which lines are broken up (slight pause at the end of a line; longer pause for a punctuation mark) and on the contrast between the passive speaker—examined, taken underground, baited—and the man of action, Clifford Hill. Again, remember that studying a text and experimenting with different ways of presenting it aloud can aid in the development of articulation, verbal confidence and variety.

"First Practice" can be the source of some lively improvisations.

1. Start, as usual, with the obvious dramatic re-creation. (What happens after the coach's sinister

signal, "*Now*," will need to be suggested in an unrealistic, perhaps ritualized way—slow motion?—rather than enacted, unless the group doesn't mind getting stomped!) *C* is Clifford Hill, and the rest are the novices. To familiarize themselves with the situation, the group might want to pantomime while an observer reads the poem; extemporized speeches and exchanges could then be added. *C* could eventually arrive at a much expanded version of Hill's ominous introduction, one that cows his captive audience even more. Discussion should include the uses and abuses of instructional authority.

2. One of the players tries to show his instinctive dismay over the whole business without getting himself into too much trouble. Depending upon the effectiveness of his reaction, the others either back him up in whatever way they can or ostracize him. The possible responses of Hill, of course, cannot be forgotten in all of this. Perhaps the commotion will lead to a confrontation between the coach and his rebellious fledgling(s). One possibility for discussion: the rights and responsibilities of students.

3. The group enacts a nightmare of Clifford Hill that is set in a classroom environment. This will demand a greater amount of advance preparation and a more than usual stretching of the collective imagination. What would a Clifford Hill classroom nightmare be like? Have two Hills: one an active participant in the dream; the other his observing, commenting consciousness.

CHARLES DICKENS,
HARD TIMES (1854)

Charles Dickens begins his great novel *Hard Times* with a short chapter called "The One Thing Needful," an allusion to Luke 10:42, when Jesus says, " 'But one thing is needful; and Mary hath chosen that good part which shall not be taken away from her.' " That one thing is faith in Christ; however, in the industrialized society Dickens portrays, the new religion of Benthamite utilitarianism has replaced religious faith with Facts. So affirms Thomas Gradgrind, self-important man of affairs, as he preaches in "a plain, bare, monotonous vault of a schoolroom."[17]

> "Now, what I want is, Facts. Teach these boys and girls nothing but Facts. Facts alone are wanted in life. Plant nothing else, and root out everything else. You can only form the minds of reasoning animals upon Facts: nothing else will ever be of any service to them. This is the principle on which I bring up my own children, and this is the principle on which I bring up these children. Stick to Facts, sir!"

> The scene was a plain, bare, monotonous vault of a schoolroom, and the speaker's square forefinger emphasized his observations by underscoring every sentence with a line on the schoolmaster's sleeve. The emphasis was helped by the speaker's square wall of a forehead, which had his eyebrows for its base, while his eyes found commodious cellarage in two dark caves, overshadowed by the wall. The emphasis was helped by the speaker's mouth, which was wide, thin,

[17]Charles Dickens, *Hard Times,* ed. David Craig (New York: Penguin, 1969), p. 47. All quotations are from the first two chapters, which are reproduced without abridgment (pp. 47–53).

and hard set. The emphasis was helped by the speaker's voice, which was inflexible, dry, and dictatorial. The emphasis was helped by the speaker's hair, which bristled on the skirts of his bald head, a plantation of firs to keep the wind from its shining surface, all covered with knobs, like the crust of a plum pie, as if the head had scarcely warehouse-room for the hard facts stored inside. The speaker's obstinate carriage, square coat, square legs, square shoulders—nay, his very neckcloth, trained to take him by the throat with an unaccommodating grasp, like a stubborn fact, as it was—all helped the emphasis.

"In this life, we want nothing but Facts, sir; nothing but Facts!"

The speaker, and the schoolmaster, and the third grown person present, all backed a little, and swept with their eyes the inclined plane of little vessels then and there arranged in order, ready to have imperial gallons of facts poured into them until they were full to the brim.

Those "little vessels" are the young students.

The next chapter shows the highly regimented system of education that grows out of this Philosophy of Fact over "Fancy" (Imagination). The chapter is called "Murdering the Innocents."

Thomas Gradgrind, sir. A man of realities. A man of fact and calculations. A man who proceeds upon the principle that two and two are four, and nothing over, and who is not to be talked into allowing for anything over. Thomas Gradgrind, sir—peremptorily Thomas— Thomas Gradgrind. With a rule and a pair of scales, and the multiplication table always in his pocket, sir, ready to weigh and measure any parcel of human nature, and tell you exactly what it comes to. It is a mere question of figures, a case of simple arithmetic.

You might hope to get some other nonsensical belief into the head of George Gradgrind, or Augustus Gradgrind, or John Gradgrind, or Joseph Gradgrind (all supposititious, nonexistent persons), but into the head of Thomas Gradgrind—no, sir!

In such terms Mr. Gradgrind always mentally introduced himself, whether to his private circle of acquaintance, or to the public in general. In such terms, no doubt, substituting the words "boys and girls," for "sir," Thomas Gradgrind now presented Thomas Gradgrind to the little pitchers before him, who were to be filled so full of facts.

Indeed, as he eagerly sparkled at them from the cellarage before mentioned, he seemed a kind of cannon loaded to the muzzle with facts, and prepared to blow them clean out of the regions of childhood at one discharge. He seemed a galvanizing apparatus, too, charged with a grim mechanical substitute for the tender young imaginations that were to be stormed away.

"Girl number twenty," said Mr. Gradgrind, squarely pointing with his square forefinger, "I don't know that girl. Who is that girl?"

"Sissy Jupe, sir," explained number twenty, blushing, standing up, and curtseying.

"Sissy is not a name," said Mr. Gradgrind. "Don't call yourself Sissy. Call yourself Cecilia."

"It's father as calls me Sissy, sir," returned the young girl in a trembling voice, and with another curtsey.

"Then he has no business to do it," said Mr. Gradgrind. "Tell him he mustn't. Cecilia Jupe. Let me see. What is your father?"

"He belongs to the horse-riding, if you please, sir."

Mr. Gradgrind frowned, and waved off the objectionable calling with his hand.

"We don't want to know anything about that, here. You mustn't tell us about that, here. Your father breaks horses, don't he?"

"If you please, sir, when they can get any to break, they do break horses in the ring, sir."

"You mustn't tell us about the ring, here. Very well, then. Describe your father as a horsebreaker. He doctors sick horses, I dare say?"

"Oh yes, sir."

"Very well, then. He is a veterinary surgeon, a farrier and horsebreaker. Give me your definition of a horse."

(Sissy Jupe thrown into the greatest alarm by this demand.)

"Girl number twenty unable to define a horse!" said Mr. Gradgrind, for the general behoof of all the little pitchers. "Girl number twenty possessed of no facts, in reference to one of the commonest of animals! Some boy's definition of a horse. Bitzer, yours."

The square finger, moving here and there, lighted suddenly on Bitzer, perhaps because he chanced to sit in the same ray of sunlight which, darting in at one of the bare windows of the intensely whitewashed room, irradiated Sissy. For, the boys and girls sat on the face of the inclined plane in two compact bodies, divided up the center by a narrow interval; and Sissy, being at the corner of a row on the sunny side, came in for the beginning of a sunbeam, of which Bitzer, being at the corner of a row on the other side, a few rows in advance, caught the end. But, whereas the girl was so dark-eyed and dark-haired, that she seemed to receive a deeper and more lustrous color from the sun when it shone upon her, the boy was so light-eyed and light-haired that the self-same rays appeared to draw out of him what little color he ever possessed. His cold eyes would hardly have been eyes, but for the short ends of lashes which, by bringing them into immediate contrast with something paler than themselves, expressed their form. His short-cropped hair might have been a mere continuation of the sandy freckles on his forehead and face. His skin was so unwholesomely deficient in the natural tinge, that he looked as though, if he were cut, he would bleed white.

"Bitzer," said Thomas Gradgrind. "Your definition of a horse."

"Quadruped. Graminivorous. Forty teeth, namely twenty-four grinders, four eye-teeth, and twelve incisive. Sheds coat in the spring; in marshy countries, sheds hoofs, too. Hoofs hard, but requiring to be shod with iron. Age known by marks in mouth." Thus (and much more) Bitzer.

"Now girl number twenty," said Mr. Gradgrind. "You know what a horse is."

She curtseyed again, and would have blushed deeper, if she could have blushed deeper than she had blushed all this time. Bitzer, after rapidly blinking at Thomas Gradgrind with both eyes at once, and so catching the light upon his quivering ends of lashes that they looked like the antennae of busy insects, put his knuckles to his freckled forehead, and sat down again.

The third gentleman now stepped forth. A mighty man at cutting and drying, he was; a government officer; in his way (and in most other people's too), a professed pugilist; always in training, always with a system to force down the general throat like a bolus, always to be heard of at the bar of his little Public-office, ready to fight all England. To continue in fistic phraseology, he had a genius for coming up to the scratch, wherever and whatever it was, and proving himself an ugly customer. He would go in and damage any subject whatever with his right, follow up with his left, stop, exchange, counter, bore his opponent (he always fought All England) to the ropes, and fall upon him neatly. He was certain to knock the wind out of common-sense, and render that unlucky adversary deaf to the call of time. And he had it in charge from high authority to bring about the great public-office Millennium, when Commissioners should reign upon earth.

"Very well," said this gentleman, briskly smiling, and folding his arms. "That's a horse. Now, let me ask you girls and boys, Would you paper a room with representations of horses?"

After a pause, one half of the children cried in chorus, "Yes, sir!" Upon which the other half, seeing in the gentleman's face that Yes was wrong, cried out in chorus, "No, sir!"—as the custom is, in these examinations.

"Of course, No. Why wouldn't you?"

A pause. One corpulent slow boy, with a wheezy manner of breathing, ventured the answer, Because he wouldn't paper a room at all, but would paint it.

"You *must* paper it," said Thomas Gradgrind, "whether you like it or not. Don't tell *us* you wouldn't paper it. What do you mean, boy?"

"I'll explain to you, then," said the gentleman, after another and a dismal pause, "why you wouldn't paper a room with representations of horses. Do you ever see horses walking up and down the sides of rooms in reality—in fact? Do you?"

"Yes, sir!" from one half. "No, sir!" from the other.

"Of course no," said the gentleman, with an indignant look at the wrong half. "Why, then, you are not to see anywhere, what you don't see in fact; you are not to have anywhere, what you don't have in fact. What is called Taste, is only another name for Fact."

Thomas Gradgrind nodded his approbation.

"This is a new principle, a discovery, a great discovery," said the gentleman. "Now, I'll try you again. Suppose you were going to carpet a room. Would you use a carpet having a representation of flowers upon it?"

There being a general conviction by this time that "No, sir!" was always the right answer to this gentleman, the chorus of No was very strong. Only a few feeble stragglers said Yes; among them Sissy Jupe.

"Girl number twenty," said the gentleman, smiling in the calm strength of knowledge.

Sissy blushed, and stood up.

"So you would carpet your room—or your husband's room, if you were a grown woman, and had a husband—with representations of flowers, would you," said the gentleman. "Why would you?"

"If you please, sir, I am very fond of flowers," returned the girl.

"And is that why you would put tables and chairs upon them, and have people walking over them with heavy boots?"

"It wouldn't hurt them, sir. They wouldn't crush and wither if you please, sir. They would be the pictures of what was very pretty and pleasant, and I would fancy—"

"Ay, ay, ay! But you mustn't fancy," cried the gentleman, quite elated by coming so happily to his point. "That's it! You are never to fancy."

"You are not, Cecilia Jupe," Thomas Gradgrind solemnly repeated, "to do anything of that kind."

"Fact, fact, fact!" said the gentleman. And "Fact, fact, fact!" repeated Thomas Gradgrind.

"You are to be in all things regulated and governed," said the gentleman, "by fact. We hope to have, before long, a board of fact, composed of commissioners of fact, who will force the people to be a people of fact, and of nothing but fact. You must discard the word Fancy altogether. You have nothing to do with it. You are not to have, in any object of use or ornament, what would be a contradiction in fact. You don't walk upon flowers in fact; you cannot be allowed to walk upon flowers in carpets. You don't find that foreign birds and butterflies come and perch upon your crockery. You never meet with quadrupeds going up and down walls; you must not have quadruped represented upon walls. You must use," said the gentleman, "for all these purposes, combinations and modifications (in primary colors) of mathematical figures which are susceptible of proof and demonstration. This is the new discovery. This is fact. This is taste."

The girl curtseyed, and sat down. She was very young, and she looked as if she were frightened by the matter of fact prospect the world afforded.

"Now, if Mr. M'Choakumchild," said the gentleman, "will proceed to give his first lesson here, Mr. Gradgrind, I shall be happy, at your request, to observe his mode of procedure."

Mr. Gradgrind was much obliged. "Mr. M'Choakumchild, we only wait for you."

So, Mr. M'Choakumchild began in his best manner. He and some one hundred and forty other schoolmasters, had been lately turned at the same time, in the same factory, on the same principles, like so many pianoforte legs. He had been put through an immense variety of paces, and had answered volumes of head-breaking questions. Orthography, etymology, syntax, and prosody, biography, astronomy, geography, and general cosmography, the sciences of compound proportion, algebra, land-surveying and leveling, vocal music, and drawing from models, were all at the ends of his ten chilled fingers. He had worked his stony way into Her Majesty's most Honorable Privy Council's Schedule B, and had taken the bloom off the higher branches of mathematics and physical science, French, German, Latin, and Greek. He knew all about all the Water Sheds of all the world (whatever they are), and all the histories of all the peoples, and all the names of all the rivers and mountains, and all the productions, manners, and customs of all the countries, and all their boundaries and bearings on the two and thirty points of the compass. Ah, rather overdone, M'Choakumchild. If he had only learnt a little less, how infinitely better he might have taught much more!

He went to work in this preparatory lesson, not unlike Morgiana in the Forty Thieves: looking into all the vessels ranged before him, one after another, to see what they contained. Say, good M'Choakumchild. When from thy boiling store, thou shalt fill each jar brim full by and by, dost thou think that thou wilt always kill outright the robber Fancy lurking within— or sometimes only maim him and distort him!

The English scholar David Craig gives us some historical background:

The fact is that the first two chapters of the novel are an almost straight copy of the teaching system in schools run by the two societies for educating the poor. In the Manchester Lancasterian School a thousand children were taught in one huge room, controlled by a kind of military drill with monitors and a monitor-general, and taught by methods derived from the Catechism. Groups of facts, mechanically classified, were drummed in by methods that might have been meant to squash forever the children's urge to find out or understand anything for themselves. . . .[18]

It would be unfair and unrealistic to suppose that we have left far behind this primitive mode of instruction. Many teachers still succumb today to the tempt-

[18]David Craig, Introd., *Hard Times,* by Charles Dickens (New York: Penguin Books, 1969), p. 22. Introduction and Notes copyright © David Craig, 1969. Reprinted by permission of Penguin Books Ltd.

ing assumption that those faces out there are really just the tops of "little pitchers . . . to be filled so full of facts"; that teaching is a one-way process requiring nothing but obedient passivity from the students, who are ciphers needing periodic shots of information. Although widespread, the assumption is obviously simplistic and even destructive. We are not arguing for the opposite extreme that reduces the teacher to pal and gentle observer; we are merely calling attention to the truth that respecting students as individuals, stimulating their interests, and guiding their active participation are all elements of effective teaching.

Reading aloud can be a powerful stimulant, and you cannot find a richer source for dramatic readings than the works of Charles Dickens. Dickens himself gave enormously popular public readings of his works in both England and America (he threw himself into these so intensely that they ultimately precipitated his death). Today, there are amateur clubs devoted to reading his novels aloud, specific members being responsible for the various major characters. In the excerpt from *Hard Times*, you will need to speak in five distinct voices—good practice for flexibility and range. Dickens gives us a stage direction for Gradgrind's voice, when he describes it in chapter one as "inflexible, dry, and dictatorial." He also helps us with Sissy Jupe's: she is "blushing" (our speech patterns change when we're embarrassed) and frightened ("in a trembling voice"). As for Bitzer, there is no explicit account of the way he sounds, but Dickens's wonderful description of the way he *looks* (". . . as though, if he were cut, he would bleed white") should give us some clues. Finally, there are the voices of the "cutting and drying" government officer and the narrator.

If you are not ready to take on by yourself a reading that involves more than one voice, regard chapters one and two as a kind of script, complete with dialogue and stage directions. First of all, there is the disembodied narrative voice connecting and commenting on the players' lines. Then there are five characters: Gradgrind, Sissy Jupe, Bitzer, the nameless government officer, and the schoolmaster, Mr. M'Choakumchild. Although he has no lines, M'Choakumchild can be the focus of an improvisation based on what Dickens tells us about his background and his first lesson, which is "not unlike Morgiana in the Forty Thieves: looking into all the vessels ranged before him, one after another, to see what they contained." Finally, there must be the anonymous members of the class, crying "Yes, sir!" and "No, sir!" and being otherwise manipulated by the all-knowing educators. A dramatized version of "The One Thing Needful" and "Murdering the Innocents" (actually, the chapters are already close to the dramatic mode) compels the participants to think about the attitudes towards education that are expressed both directly and indirectly through Dickens's words and to experience imaginatively the consequences of those attitudes. It can also be great fun.

Besides the M'Choakumchild improvisation already mentioned, there are other possibilities. As with all the other suggestions for improvisations, these are certainly not comprehensive. Additional ideas are up to you.

1. Take the Gradgrind approach with a particular subject. In other words, the teacher chooses a

lecture topic and treats it exactly as Gradgrind would. This does not mean that he or she must try to *become* Gradgrind and enact the character, but instead that the teacher operate on the cardinal principle: "In this life, we want nothing but Facts, sir; nothing but Facts!"

2. Have a class full of Bitzers, each one more eager than the next to please the teacher with a whole mess of facts.

BEL KAUFMAN, *UP THE DOWN STAIRCASE* (1964)

Years after its original publication, Bel Kaufman's novel remains one of the best accounts of the frustrations and rewards that come with teaching at a big, bureaucratic urban high school. The four chapters we include here, like the first two of Dickens's *Hard Times,* are cast in a form that is practical for both improvisation and performance based on a script.[19]

Hi, teach!
Looka *her!* She's a teacher?
Who she?
Is this 304? Are you Mr. Barringer?
No. I'm Miss Barrett.
I'm supposed to have Mr. Barringer.
I'm Miss Barrett.
You the teacher? You so young.
Hey she's cute! Hey, teach, can I be in your class?

[19]Bel Kaufman, *Up the Down Staircase* (Englewood Cliffs, N.J.: Prentice-Hall, 1964), pp. 3–12, 191–93, 205–09, and 339–40 (Chapters 1, 30, 34, and 58). Reprinted by permission of Bel Kaufman.

Please don't block the doorway. Please come in.
    Good afternoon, Miss Barnet.
Miss Barrett. My name is on the blackboard. Good morning.
    O, no! A *dame* for homeroom?
    You want I should slug him, teach?
    Is this homeroom period?
Yes. Sit down, please.
    I don't belong here.
    We gonna have you all term? Are you a regular or
a sub?
    There's not enough chairs!
Take any seat at all.
    Hey, where do we sit?
    Is this 309?
    Someone swiped the pass. Can I have a pass?
    What's your name?
My name is on the board.
    I can't read your writing.
    I gotta go to the nurse. I'm dying.
    Don't believe him, teach. He ain't dying!
    Can I sharpen my pencil in the office?
    Why don't you leave the teacher alone, you bums?
    Can we sit on the radiator? That's what we did last
term.
    Hi, teach! You the homeroom?
    Pipe down, you morons! Don't you see the teacher's
trying to say something?
Please sit down. I'd like to——
    Hey, the bell just rung!
    How come Mrs. Singer's not here? She was in this
room last term.
    When do we go home?
    The first day of school, he wants to go home
already!
That bell is your signal to come to order. Will you please——

Can I have a pass to a drink of water?

You want me to alphabetize for you?

What room is this?

This is room 304. My name is on the board: Miss Barrett. I'll have you for homeroom all term, and I hope to meet some of you in my English classes. Now, someone once said that first impressions——

English! No wonder!

Who needs it?

You give homework?

First impressions, they say, are lasting. What do we base our first——Yes? Do you belong in this class?

No. Mr. McHabe wants Ferone right away.

Who?

McHabe.

Whom does he want?

Joe Ferone.

Is Joe Ferone here?

Him? That's a laugh!

He'll show up when he feels like it.

Put down that window-pole, please. We all know that first impressions——Yes?

Is this 304?

Yes. You're late.

I'm not late. I'm absent.

You are?

I was absent all last term.

Well—sit down.

I can't. I'm dropping out. You're supposed to sign my Book Clearance from last term.

Do you owe any books?

I'm not on the Blacklist! That's a yellow slip. This here is a green!

Hey, isn't the pass back yet?

Quit your shoving!

He started it, teach!

I'd like you to come to order, please. I'm afraid we won't have time for the discussion on first impressions I had planned. I'm passing out——

Hey, she's passing out!

Give her air!

——Delaney cards. You are to fill them out at once while I take attendance from the Roll Book. Standees—line up in back of the room; you may lean on the wall to write. Print, in ink, your last name first, your parent's name, your date of birth, your address, my name—it's on the board—and the same upside down. I'll make out a seating plan in the Delaney Book. Any questions?

In ink or pencil?

I got no ink—can I use pencil? Who's got a pencil to loan me?

I don't remember when I was born.

Don't mind him—he's a comic.

Print or write?

When do we go to lunch?

I can't write upside down!

Ha-ha. He kills me laughing!

What do you need my address for? My father can't come.

Someone robbed my ball-point!

I can't do it—I lost my glasses.

Are these going to be our regular seats—the *radiator?*

I don't know my address—we're moving.

Where are you moving?

I don't know where.

Where do you live?

I don't live no place.

Any place. *You, young man, why are you late?*
    I'm not even here. I'm in Mr. Loomis. My uncle's in this class. He forgot his lunch. Hi, Tony—catch!
Please don't throw——Yes, what is it?
    This Mrs. Singer's room?
Yes. No. Not anymore.
    Anyone find a sneaker from last term?
    Hey, teach, can we use a pencil?
    You want these filled out *now?*
    There's chewing gum on my seat!
    First name last or last name first?
    I *gotta* have a pass to the Men's Room. I know my rights; this is a democracy, ain't it?
Isn't. What's the trouble now?
    There's glass all over my desk from the window.
Please don't do that. Don't touch that broken window. It should be reported to the custodian. Does anyone——
    I'll go!
    Me! Let *me* go! That's Mr. Grayson—I know where he is in the basement!
All right. Tell him it's urgent. And who are you?
    I'm sorry I'm late. I was in Detention.
The what?
    The Late Room. Where they make you sit to make up your lateness when you come late.
All right, sit down. I mean, stand up—over there, against the wall.
    For parent's name, can I use my aunt?
Put down your mother's name.
    I got no mother.
Well—do the best you can. Yes, young lady?
    The office sent me. Read this to your class and sign here.

May I have your attention, please. Please, class! There's been a change in today's assembly schedule. Listen carefully:

PLEASE IGNORE PREVIOUS INSTRUCTIONS IN CIRCULAR #3, PARAGRAPHS 5 AND 6, AND FOLLOW THE FOLLOWING:

THIS MORNING THERE WILL BE A LONG HOME-ROOM PERIOD EXTENDING INTO THE FIRST HALF OF THE SECOND PERIOD. ALL X2 SECTIONS ARE TO REPORT TO ASSEMBLY THE SECOND HALF OF THE SECOND PERIOD. FIRST PERIOD CLASSES WILL BEGIN THE FOURTH PERIOD, SECOND PERIOD CLASSES WILL BEGIN THE FIFTH PERIOD, THIRD PERIOD CLASSES WILL BEGIN THE SIXTH PERIOD, AND SO ON, SUBJECT CLASSES BEING SHORTENED TO 23 MINUTES IN LENGTH, EXCEPT LUNCH, WHICH WILL BE NORMAL.

I can't hear you—what did you say?
They're drilling on the street!
Close the window.
I can't—I'll suffocate!
This a long homeroom?
What's today's date?
It's September, stupid!
Your attention, please. I'm not finished:

SINCE IT IS DIFFICULT TO PROVIDE ADEQUATE SEATING SPACE FOR ALL STUDENTS UNDER EXISTING FACILITIES, THE OVERFLOW IS TO STAND IN THE AISLES UNTIL THE SALUTE TO THE FLAG AND THE *STAR-SPANGLED BANNER* ARE COMPLETED, AFTER WHICH THE OVERFLOW MAY BE DIRECTED FROM THE PLATFORM. THIS IS A FIRE LAW. DR. CLARKE WILL EXTEND A WARM WELCOME TO ALL NEW STU-

DENTS; HIS TOPIC WILL BE "OUR CULTURAL HERITAGE." ANY STUDENT FOUND TALKING OR EATING LUNCH IN ASSEMBLY IS TO BE REPORTED AT ONCE TO MR. McHABE.

Water! I gotta have water! My throat is parching! He thinks he's funny?
May I have your attention?
No!

TOMORROW ALL Y2 SECTIONS WILL FOLLOW TODAY'S PROGRAM FOR X2 SECTIONS WHILE ALL X2 SECTIONS WILL FOLLOW TODAY'S PROGRAM FOR Y2 SECTIONS.

Where do we go?
What period is this?
The two boys in the back—stop throwing that board eraser. Please come to order; there's more:
Is this assembly day?

BE SURE TO USE THE ROWS ASSIGNED TO YOU: THERE IS TO BE NO SUBSTITUTION.

Excuse me, I'm from Guidance. Miss Friedenberg wants Joe Ferone right away.
He isn't here. Will you pass your Delaney cards down, please, while I——
I didn't start yet! I'm waiting for the pen.
How do you spell your name?
Hey, he threw the board eraser out the window!
Here's my admit. He says I was loitering.
Who?
McHabe.
Mr. McHabe.

Either way.
Now class, please finish your Delaney cards while I call the roll.
I didn't finish!
I never got no Delaney!
Any. Yes?
Mr. Manheim next door wants to borrow your board eraser.
I'm afraid it's gone. Please, *class* ——
You give extra credit for alphabetizing?
We go to assembly today?
You want me to go down for the stuff from your letter-box, Miss Barnet?
All right. Now we'll just have to ——
I can't write—I got a bum hand.
You gonna be our teacher?
Please come to order while I take attendance. And correct me if I mispronounce your name; I know how annoying that can be. I hope to get to know all of you soon. Abrams, Harry?
Here.
Quiet, please, so I can hear you. Allen, Frank?
Absent.
Absent?
He ain't here.
Isn't. Amdur, Janet?
Here.
Mr. Grayson says there's no one down there.
How can he say that when he's there?
That's what he says. Any answer?
No. Amdur, Janet?
I was here already.
Arbuzzi, Vincent? Yes, what do I have to sign now?
Nothing. I came back from the bathroom.
Can I have the pass?

Me, I'm next!

I said it first!

Blake, Alice?

I'm present, Miss Barrett.

Blanca, Carmelita?

Carole. I changed my name.

Blanca, Carole?

Here.

Borden——Yes?

Miss Finch wants you to make this out right away.

I'm in the middle of taking attendance. Borden——

She needs it right away.

Excuse me, class.

IN THE TWO COLUMNS LABELED MALE AND
FEMALE, INDICATE THE NUMBER OF STUDENTS
IN YOUR HOMEROOM SECTION BORN BE-
TWEEN THE FOLLOWING DATES—

*Please don't tilt that chair——Boy in the back—I'm talking to
you——Oh!*

So I fell. Big deal. Stop laughing, you bums, or I'll
knock your brains out!

Are you hurt?

Naw, just my head.

You've got to make out an accident report, Miss
Barrett, three copies, and send him to the nurse.

Aw, she ain't even allowed to give out aspirins.
Only tea.

Get your feet offa me!

You call this a *chair?*

He can sue the whole Board of Education!

*Perhaps you'd better go to the nurse. And ask her for the
accident report blanks. Yes, what can I do for you?*

Miss Friedenberg wants last term's Service Credit cards.

I wasn't here last term. And what do you want?

Miss Finch is waiting for the attendance reports and absentee cards.

I'm in the middle of——Yes?

The office wants to know are the transportation cards ready?

The what cards?

Bus and subway.

No. Yes?

You're supposed to read this to the class. It's from the liberry.

Library. May I have your attention, please?

THE SCHOOL LIBRARY IS *YOUR* LIBRARY. ALL STUDENTS ARE ENCOURAGED TO USE IT AT ALL TIMES.

STUDENTS ON THE LIBRARY BLACKLIST ARE NOT TO RECEIVE THEIR PROGRAM CARDS UNTIL THEY HAVE PAID FOR LOST OR MUTILATED BOOKS.

THE LIBRARY WILL BE CLOSED TO STUDENTS UNTIL FURTHER NOTICE TO ENABLE TEACHERS TO USE IT AS A WORKROOM FOR THEIR PRC ENTRIES.

Yes, who sent you here?

You did. Here's the stuff from your letter-box. Where do I dump it?

Is that all for me?

Excuse me, the nurse says she's all out of accident reports, but she wants the missing dentals.

The missing what?

Dental notes.

I see. And what is it you want?
New change in assembly program. Your class goes to different rows. X2 schedule rows.
I see. And you?
Mr. McHabe says do you need any posters for your room decoration?
Tell Mr. McHabe what I really need is——Yes?
The office wants the list of locker numbers for each student.
I haven't even——Yes?
This is urgent. You're supposed to read and sign.

TO ALL TEACHERS: A BLUE PONTIAC PARKED IN FRONT OF SCHOOL HAS BEEN OVERTURNED BY SOME STUDENTS. IF THE FOLLOWING LICENSE IS YOURS—

Tell Mr. McHabe I don't drive. Now, class——
Hurray! Saved by the bell!
Just a minute—the bell seems to be fifteen minutes early. It may be a mistake. We have so much to—— Please remain in your——
That's the *bell!* You heard it!
All the other teachers are letting them out!
But we must finish the ——
When the bell rings, we're supposed to *go!*
Where do we go, assembly?
Please sit down. I'd like to——We haven't——Well. It looks as if you and I are the only ones left. Your name is——?
Alice Blake, Miss Barrett. I just wanted you to know how much I enjoyed your lesson.
Thank you, but it wasn't really a——Yes, young lady?
I'm from the office. She says to announce this to your class right away.

PLEASE DISREGARD THE BELLS. STUDENTS ARE
TO REMAIN IN THEIR HOMEROOMS UNTIL THE
WARNING BELL RINGS.

I'm afraid they've all gone.

I've got to go too, Miss Barrett. I wish I had *you*
for English, but my program says Mr. Barringer.

*I'm sure he's a fine teacher, Alice, and that you'll do well with
him.*

You Barrett?

What's that, young man?

Late pass.

*That's no way to hand it to me. Throwing it like that on my
desk——*

My aim is bad.

*There's no need for insolence. Please take that toothpick out of
your mouth when you talk to me. And take your hands out of
your pockets.*

Which first?

What's your name?

You gonna report me?

What's your name?

You gonna give me a zero?

I'm afraid I've had just about——What's your name?

Joe.

Joe what?

Ferone. You gonna send a letter home? Take
away my lollipop? Lecture me? Spank me?

All I asked——

Yeah. All you asked.

I don't allow anyone to talk to me like that.

So you're lucky—you're a teacher!

*   *   *   *   *

Fri., Nov. 6

Dear Ellen,

I rejoice with you at the departure of the painters. What do you mean, it came out buff?

You're right; I *am* attracted to Paul. He's very attractive. But the surface is so highly polished, it's hard to get hold of it. One slips off. Our relationship is surface too: an occasional drink together, a dinner, a movie in my "spare time, Ha-ha!"—as one of my kids would say. I smile at his amusing verses and I listen to his amused complaints about editors and school and fate. He's a kind of charming Minniver Cheevy—without the bathos. I'd like to like him more.

As for your questions: Yes, Linda Rosen is back, presumably cured. So is Joe Ferone, presumably not. He has changed his mind about seeing me after school. "What's in it for you?" he asks.

The day he returned to class, with a Late-Late pass from McHabe, who detained him for coming late (do you follow me?) I was observed by Bester. I taught a poem. Or did I? I don't think I got through to them, in spite of all my careful paper-plans, in spite of all of Bester's paper-words.

The trouble is their utter lack of background. "I never read a book in my life, and I ain't starting now," a boy informed me. It isn't easy to make them *like* a book—other teachers got there before me. Henrietta with her games in teams, Mary with her outlines. Or perhaps it goes further back, to the 1st grade, or the 5th?

The important thing is to make them feel King Lear's anguish, not a True-or-False test on Shakespeare. The important thing is the recognition and response, not an inch of print to be memorized.

I want to point the way to something that should forever lure them, when the TV set is broken and the movie is over and the school bell has rung for the last time.

But what a book report means to them is: to tell an interesting fact about the author ("Poe was a junkie"); to complete: "This book made me wish/ wonder/ realize/ decide"; to recount one humorous/ tragic incident; or to engage in hokum projects such as designing book jackets, drawing stick figures, holding TV interviews with dead authors or imaginary characters, playing "Who Am I?," and pepping up the classics. In other words, saving the others the trouble of reading the book.

Sample:

Lou: My book is——
I: The book you read.
Lou: Yeah. The title is called *Macbeth* by Shakespeare.
I: Its title *is*.
Lou: *Macbeth*.
I: But wasn't it required reading for last term's English? I understand *Macbeth* was taught in English 2 last term. You were supposed to report on a supplementary book. That means, in addition to the required——
Lou: I ain't never read it before.
I: I never read it.
Lou: Me neither. In this book the author depicks—
I: Depicts.
Lou: Depicks how this guy he wants to——
I: Who?
Lou: Him.
I: He.

Lou: Yeah. He potrays that this here——
I: He *says*.
Lou: Mrs. Lewis told us not to say say. She gave us a whole list like depicks and potrays instead.
I: Yes, Harry?
Harry: Observes.
I: I beg your pardon?
Harry: Remarks. Narrates. Exclaims. I've got it written down.
I: She probably wanted you to avoid repetition. There's nothing wrong with the word "says." What's the theme of the play, Lou?
Lou: Well, the author narrates this murder——
I: No, the theme, not the plot. Does anyone know the difference between theme and plot? Linda?
Linda: The plot is what they do in the book and the theme is how they do it.
I: Not exactly. The theme——Yes, Vivian?
Vivian: The theme is what's behind it.
I: Behind what?
Vivian: The plot.
I: Frank?
Frank: The lesson.
I: What lesson? Please answer in complete sentences.
Frank: That the author is trying to teach. The morale of the book.
I: The moral. It need not——Yes, John?
John: He's supposed to mention three incidents.
I: But we're talking about the——Harry?
Harry: Personal opinion.
I: What?
Harry: He didn't give his personal opinion.
Lou: I didn't even get to it.

I: We're still trying to determine the difference between plot and theme. Sally?

Sally: One is real and one is made up.

I: Well, actually—Yes, Carole, what is it?

Carole: Oh, thank God! I thought you'd never call on me! The author tries to say——

I: Tries? Doesn't he succeed?

Carole: He tries to show——

I: He shows.

Carole: He shows how you mustn't be ambitious.

Lou: Potrays.

I: Does he say that ambition is bad?

Carole: Yes.

I: *Is* it? Isn't it good to be ambitious? Lou?

Lou: It's good, but not too.

I: Not too what?

Lou: Not too ambitious is not so good.

I: You mean, excessive ambition can lead to disaster?

Lou: That's right.

I: Why don't you say it? The theme of *Macbeth* is that excessive—or rather, ruthless ambition often proves disastrous. That's what words are for—to be used. What does ruthless mean? Eddie?

Eddie: Steps all over.

I: Say it in a sentence.

Eddie: He steps all over.

I: Rusty, you wanted to say something?

Rusty: Mrs. Macbeth noodges him.

I: You mean nudges?

Rusty: Noodges. Being a female, she spurns him on.

I: Yes, John, your hand is up?

John: I read the same book, but my theme is different.

I: What is it?

John: The theme is he kills him for his own good.

Never mind. I may be reaching too high, I may stumble and fall, but I'll keep on trying!

Love,
Syl

P.S. Did you know that at the College Entrance Examination Board's Commission on English it was found that a third of high school English teachers were unfit to teach their subject?

S.

*   *   *   *   *

Nov. 12

Dear Ellen,

Just got home from Open School session—and I *must* talk to someone!

It was a fiasco, though I did everything I was told to do. I got fresh book jackets from the library to festoon the walls with and had my wardrobe cleaned out. (Why is it only *one* sneaker is always left on the closet floor? And the ubiquitous, tattered notebook? I found one belonging to one of my homeroom girls, Alice Blake, full of scribbles, doodles, and chaos.) I even made sure that the little flag stuck in the radiator, which we salute each morning before singing the Calvin Coolidge Alma Mater ("Ye loyal sons and daughters"—a substitute for the unlawful hymns) was tilted at the correct angle. (The other day Admiral Ass found it drooping disrespectfully.)

I see 243 kids daily: 201 in English (after dropouts and new registers) and 42 in homeroom—but only a few parents showed up; a few wrote cards; and the rest ignored the whole thing. The ones I had particularly hoped to see never came.

I don't know why they hold Open School so soon after the beginning of the term, before we've had time to get to know all our students. The Delaney Book wasn't much help to me; it showed days absent, times late, and some checks, crosses and zeroes—I'd forgotten for what. Unprepared homework? An insolent whistle? A four-letter word?

One father came, in work overalls, hands patiently clasped on the desk, out of some dim memory of his own school days. The mothers—patient, used to waiting, careworn, timid, bewildered or just curious—sat clutching their pocketbooks, waiting to plead, appease, complain or hear a kind word. A few were hostile and belligerent; they had come to avenge themselves on their own teachers of long ago, or demand special privileges, or ask the teacher to do the job they had failed to do.

And I—who was I to tell these grown-ups anything about their children? What did I know? A few clichés from the mimeographed directives: "Works to capacity, doesn't work to capacity, fine boy, fine girl." A few euphemisms: "Seems to enjoy school" (the guffawer); "Is quite active" (the window-smasher) . . .

For a moment, the notion occurred to me to try to match the parent to the child; but they were strangers, looking at me with opaque eyes.

Mother: How's my boy doing?
I: What's his name?
Mother: Jim.
I: Jim what?

Mother: Stobart.

I: Oh, yes. (Now, which one was he?) Well, let's see now. (Open the Delaney Book with an air of authority: a quick glance—no help. Stobart? Was he the boy who kept drumming with a pencil on his desk? Or the short, rosy one who reclined in his tilted chair combing his hair all the time? Or the one who never removed his jacket? I couldn't find his Delaney card; perhaps his mother would give me a clue.)

Mother: About that F you gave him.

I: Oh, yes. Well, he's obviously not working to capacity. (He must be the boy who got an F on his composition, on which he had written only one sentence: "I was too absent to do it".) He must work harder.

Mother: Pass him, and he won't do it again.

I: I'm afraid that's no solution. He simply isn't using his potential.

Mother: You mean he's dumb?

I: Oh, no!

Mother: He's afraid to open his mouth. Smack him, just smack him one.

I: He should volunteer more.

Mother: I tried my best. (Helplessness, shame in her voice—and were there tears in her eyes?) Do me a favor—pass him.

I: Why do you think he is doing so poorly?

Mother: *You're* the teacher!

I: He seems to be just coasting along.

Mother: He can't help it, he was born premature. He won't do it again.

I: Well, it's a good thing that we are both concerned; perhaps, with more encouragement at home? Can his father——

Mother: That son of a bitch bastard I hope he rots in hell I haven't seen him in six years (said in the same apologetic, soft pleading tone).

I: Well (five minutes are up, by my watch), it's been a pleasure to meet you. (But she doesn't go.) Is there something else?

Mother: (Those weren't tears; anger is filming her eyes.) What does it cost you to pass him? No skin off your hide!

I: I'm afraid his work doesn't warrant——

Mother: Do me a favor, at least keep him in after school. I can't take it no more.

I: I'm afraid that's impossible; you see——

Mother: But you're the *teacher!* He'll listen to a *teacher!*

I: We can both try to make him work harder, but he has so many absences——

Mother: Maybe if you made Physics more understandable to him he would come more.

I: Physics? I teach English!

Mother: How come?

I: What room were you supposed to be in?

Mother: 306, Mrs. Manheim.

I: I'm afraid there's been a misunderstanding. *Mr.* Manheim is the man you want to see. I'm Miss Barrett, Room 304.

Mother: Well, why didn't you say so?

Still, I learned a few things. I learned that the reason a student failed to bring his father's signature is that the father is in jail; that the Federal Lunch the kids are always griping about is often the only meal they have; that the boy who falls asleep in class works all night in a garage in order to buy a sports car; that the girl who had neglected to do her homework had no place to do it in.

I have a long way to go.

In the meantime, write, write soon. You too bring me a glimpse of "real life." One can get as ingrown as a toenail here.

Love,
Syl

P.S. Did you know that due to the "high mobility" of families unable to pay rent, some schools have a turnover of 100% between September and June?

S

NOVEMBER 13

TO: ALL TEACHERS
YOU ARE TO BE CONGRATULATED AND COMMENDED ON THE COMPLETE AND UNQUALIFIED SUCCESS OF OPEN SCHOOL YESTERDAY. IT IS THROUGH PARENT-TEACHER CONFERENCES SUCH AS THESE THAT CLOSER COMMUNICATION BETWEEN THE SCHOOL, AND THE HOME CAN BE EFFECTUATED AND ACHIEVED.

MAXWELL E. CLARKE,
PRINCIPAL

*   *   *   *   *

Is this 304?
Hey, she's back!
You out of the hospital?
Hurray, we got Barrett!
How's your foot?
Let's give her a round of clap!
Thank you for the applause, but that's enough. That's <u>enough</u>, thank you. I'm glad to see you again too. And now, please fill out these Delaney cards while I call the roll——

What's the date?

February first, you moron!

There's not enough seats!

Hey, we got a lot of new kids here!

I'm not late—the bell is early.

You gonna be our English too?

Is Lou Martin here? Oh, there you are.

Who, *me?* I didn't do it! Honest—cross my——

Stop clowning, Lou. I just want you to know you were right.
You were absolutely right.

You got a cold?

Who's got a pen to loan me?

You want my Kleenex?

Quit pushing!

I don't need a Delaney, I'm dropping out.

See me after school, and we'll talk about it.

Can I have a pass? I've got to leave the room—I've
got a doctor's note to prove it!

Hey, the window's broke!

Pipe down, you guys, you know she means business!

Acevedo, Fiore?

Here.

Adamson, Ruth?

Here.

Please *come to order. I can't hear you when you—— Put that*
chair down! Amdur, Janet?

Here.

Good morning, Rusty. Why are you late?

I'm not late—I had my English changed. I wanted
you.

I'm glad. Well—find a place to stand. Axelrod, Leon?——No,
don't bother me with these circulars until I'm through with
attendance. Axelrod, Leon? Is he absent?

Him? He's always absent!

You're lucky he's not here!
Boy, will he give you trouble!
Hey, I'm too crowded!
My desk is full of holes!
Is this the right room?
Hi, teach!
Hi, pupe! . . . Belgado, Ramos?

*   *   *   *   *

Some exercises readily suggest themselves:

1. On your own, read aloud those chaotic homeroom sessions or the book report scene and see how many different attitudes you can signify, vocally and facially. Don't rush through them; read at *half* the speed that the words would actually be spoken.

2. With a colleague, perform the mother-teacher dialogue, either memorized or read. The parenthetical material for Miss Barrett provides an interesting counterpoint to what is actually said.

EUGÈNE IONESCO, THE LESSON (1951)

Eugène Ionesco's playlet *The Lesson,* first produced in Paris in 1951, should be read by anyone interested in the craft of teaching.[20] A nightmarish vision of the

[20]Eugène Ionesco, *The Lesson,* in *Four Plays,* trans. Donald M. Allen (New York: Grove Press, 1958). [The two excerpts are taken from p. 46 and pp. 74–75.] Reprinted by permission of Grove Press, Inc. Copyright © 1958 by Grove Press, Inc.

student-teacher relationship, it concerns a private lesson between the Professor (fifty to sixty years old) and the Young Pupil (a young lady of eighteen or so), which takes place in the Professor's home. At the beginning, the Professor—"a little old man with a little white beard," according to Ionesco's stage directions—is "excessively polite, very timid, his voice deadened by his timidity, very proper, very much the teacher." The pupil is at first full of energy. As the play progresses, the actions become more and more absurd. For example, the student hopes to qualify for a doctorate but cannot master the concept of simple subtraction; the Professor finally abandons mathematics and delivers a largely incomprehensible lecture on the nature of language and languages. The most important action, however, occurs in the changes undergone by both characters. Here is how Ionesco describes these transformations:

> ... she [the pupil] becomes progressively sad and morose; from very lively at the beginning, she becomes more and more fatigued and somnolent. Towards the end of the play her face must clearly express a nervous depression; her way of speaking shows the effects of this, her tongue becomes thick, words come to her memory with difficulty and emerge from her mouth with as much difficulty; she comes to have a manner vaguely paralyzed, the beginning of aphasia. Firm and determined at the beginning, so much so as to appear to be almost aggressive, she becomes more and more passive, until she is almost a mute and inert object, seemingly inanimate in the Professor's hands, to such an extent that when he makes his final gesture, she no longer reacts. Insensible, her reflexes deadened, only her eyes in an expressionless face will show inexpressible astonishment and fear. The transition from one

manner to the other must of course be made imperceptibly.

The Professor enters. He is a little old man with a little white beard. He wears pince-nez, a black skull cap, a long black schoolmaster's coat, trousers and shoes of black, detachable white collar, a black tie. Excessively polite, very timid, his voice deadened by his timidity, very proper, very much the teacher. He rubs his hands together constantly; occasionally a lewd gleam comes into his eyes and is quickly repressed.

During the course of the play his timidity will disappear progressively, imperceptibly; and the lewd gleams in his eyes will become a steady devouring flame in the end. From a manner that is inoffensive at the start, the Professor becomes more and more sure of himself, more and more nervous, aggressive, dominating, until he is able to do as he pleases with the Pupil, who has become, in his hands, a pitiful creature. Of course, the voice of the Professor must change too, from thin and reedy, to stronger and stronger, until at the end it is extremely powerful, ringing, sonorous. . . .

At the beginning of the lesson, all seems well. The student is enthusiastic yet deferential, while the professor is delighted to discover that she has advanced in her education enough to know the capital of France. The atmosphere soon changes, however, and the learning process gradually disintegrates. His pupil grows stupider and stupider, and the professor resorts to more and more primitive pedagogical methods. At one point, the two are shouting at each other as the professor argues brutally but ineffectively that two minus one is indeed one. Finally, he begins a bewildering harangue on the distinctions between various languages. There is only one way, he decides, to teach the young woman what she must know, and that is to go over all translations of one term: "knife." His maid, Marie, appears for a moment to forestall what she foresees frightenedly, but there is no stopping him now:

Professor: Look, come on, quickly, repeat after me: "kni" . . .

Pupil: Oh, since you insist . . . knife . . . knife [*In a lucid moment, ironically:*] Is that neo-Spanish . . . ?

Professor: If you like, yes, it's neo-Spanish, but hurry up . . . we haven't got time . . . And then, what do you mean by that insidious question? What are you up to?

Pupil [*becoming more and more exhausted, weeping, desperate, at the same time both exasperated and in a trance*]: Ah!

Professor: Repeat, watch. [*He imitates a cuckoo:*] Knife, knife . . . knife, knife . . . knife, knife . . . knife, knife . . .

Pupil: Oh, my head . . . aches . . . [*With her hand she caressingly touches the parts of her body as she names them:*] . . . My eyes . . .

Professor: [*like a cuckoo*]: Knife, knife . . . knife, knife . . .

[*They are both standing. The professor still brandishes his invisible knife, nearly beside himself, as he circles around her in a sort of scalp dance, but it is important that this not be exaggerated and that his dance steps be only suggested. The Pupil stands facing the audience, then recoils in the direction of the window, sickly, languid, victimized.*]

Professor: Repeat, repeat: knife . . . knife . . . knife . . .

Pupil: I've got a pain . . . my throat, neck . . . oh, my shoulders . . . my breast . . . knife . . .

Professor: Knife . . . knife . . . knife . . .

Pupil: My hips . . . knife . . . my thighs . . . kni . . .

Professor: Pronounce it carefully . . . knife . . . knife . . .

Pupil: Knife . . . my throat . . .

Professor: Knife . . . knife . . .

Pupil: Knife . . . my shoulders . . . my arms, my breast, my hips . . . knife . . . knife . . .

Professor: That's right . . . Now, you're pronouncing it well . . .

Pupil: Knife . . . my breast . . . my stomach . . .

Professor [*changing his voice*]: Pay attention . . . don't break my window . . . the knife kills . . .

Pupil [*in a weak voice*]: Yes, yes . . . the knife kills?

Professor [*striking the Pupil with a very spectacular blow of the knife*]: Aaah! That'll teach you!

[*Pupil also cries "Aah!" then falls, flopping in an immodest position onto a chair which, as though by chance, is near the window. The murderer and his victim shout "Aaah!" at the same moment. After the first blow of the knife, the Pupil flops onto the chair, her legs spread wide and hanging over both sides of the chair. The Professor remains standing in front of her, his back to the audience. After the first blow, he strikes her dead with a second slash of the knife, from bottom to top. After that blow a noticeable convulsion shakes his whole body.*]

Professor [*winded, mumbling*]: Bitch . . . Oh, that's good, that does me good . . . Ah! Ah! I'm exhausted . . . I can scarcely breathe . . . Aah! [*He breathes with difficulty; he falls—fortunately a chair is there; he mops his brow, mumbles some incomprehensible words; his breathing becomes normal. He gets up, looks at the knife in his hand, looks at the young girl, then as though he were waking up, in a panic:*] What have I done! What's going to happen to me now! What's going to happen! Oh! dear! Oh dear, I'm in trouble! Young lady, young lady, get up! [*He is agitated, still holding onto the invisible knife, which he doesn't know what to do with.*] Come now, young lady, the lesson is over . . . you may go . . . you can pay another time . . . Oh! she is dead . . . dea-ead . . . And by my knife . . . She is dea-ead . . . It's terrible. [*He calls the Maid:*] Marie! Marie! My good Marie, come here! Ah! ah! [*The door on the right opens a little and Marie appears.*] No . . . don't come in . . . I made a mistake . . . I don't need you, Marie . . . I don't need you anymore . . . do you understand? . . .

[*Maid enters wearing a stern expression, without saying a word. She sees the corpse.*]

Professor [*in a voice less and less assured*]: I don't need you, Marie . . .

Near the play's conclusion we discover that this Young Pupil is the Professor's fortieth victim. And the final tableau brings us a ringing doorbell and the Maid greeting the forty-first.

What is one supposed to make of all this? Audience reactions to the play range from fascination to bewilderment and anger: "What the hell is Ionesco trying to say?" Well, Ionesco may not be trying to "say" anything that can be summed up apart from the experience of the play itself. As we suggested before, he is presenting us with a nightmare. Although nightmares are hardly reliable reproductions of everyday realities, they can be quite revealing about perceptions and emotions that are hidden or partially obscured by the surface of mundane appearances. Try another analogy: think of the play as one of those distorting mirrors found in fun houses. They are not accurate reflectors, but the outrageous images they create sometimes allow us to perceive aspects of ourselves we had never seen before.

Ionesco's Professor is not the only murderer we have encountered; recall the title of chapter two in *Hard Times*. *The Lesson* poses questions about what exactly goes on in the process called "teaching"; about the kinds of potentially dangerous interdependencies that may exist between student and teacher; about what George Steiner has called "the whiff of sadism" that some people notice in the academic environment.[21] Instructors do not make a habit of knifing their students. But a parasitic relationship does sometimes develop, consciously or unconsciously, in which teachers feed off students' energy, respect, insecurity, and impressionability in order to nourish their own egotism. The profession, in fact, is beset with the seeds of egotism. If we are not careful, teaching can be destructive—not only to the teacher's own sense of perspective, but also to the students' confidence and capacity for independent thinking. It is all too easy for us to circumvent student participation and just impose our knowledge from without. It is all too easy, in other words, to do their thinking for them and thus gain more power over them. Despite the conventional portrait of teachers as selfless and magnanimous (they are certainly not in it for the money, the reasoning goes), teaching is for some a most selfish activity.

The Professor in *The Lesson* turns out, for a while

[21]George Steiner, "Reflections: The Cleric of Treason," *The New Yorker,* 8 Dec. 1980, p. 188.

at least, to be someone with an unhealthy amount of power. Some teachers need to guard against the cultivation of too much power over their students; others are quite unaware of or even uncomfortable with the power they do have and do wield. What seems to one teacher only an appropriate criticism of a student might be enough to scare that student away from the class or the entire field. We forget about the pure vulnerability of many students; we unfairly take for granted a facility with the material that we have no right to expect; if students are having problems we often assume that they are lazy or stupid or both. "I'm not sure what you want for this paper assignment," the anxious student says to the college professor on the other side of that intimidating desk. "Just good writing," the professor replies disingenuously. "Right, but I'm not sure what you *want*," responds the student, who is really saying, Tell me what to do, tell me what to write, tell me what and how to *think*. That kind of immediate power and influence should not be dismissed lightly. If we do not acknowledge and respect its significance, then we become that much more limited and unaware as teachers.

The Lesson is the first actual play that we have considered in our repertoire of texts. This makes the mechanics of a dramatization relatively simple—the script is there, and any one of a number of scenes is ready to be performed—but a reading done by one person alone is more challenging. The reader must come prepared with two distinct voices, each of which undergoes substantial changes, and he must also occasionally inform the listeners about certain essential actions indicated in the stage directions. Other stage directions will not have to be read, since they can simply be incorporated into the delivery of lines. This needs to be worked out in advance, though, so that the reader is not troubled with sifting through various stage directions and deciding which need to be conveyed at the time of the reading.

So far we have avoided the complexities of a full-scale dramatization. The dramatic readings and improvisations discussed up till now demand little or nothing in the way of props, sets, or memorization. These do not seem necessary for the kinds of vocal, physical, and imaginative skills we are working on. Still, we do not want to discourage the more ambitious souls who are willing to try producing a scene. Be careful, though, not to take on more than you can handle. There are enough risks involved in just honestly coming to terms with Ionesco's startling work through one of the following ways.

1. Act out a scene from the play, with script in hand (you'll have to find a few copies). Your movements will be restricted, so focus more on suggesting as much as possible about the character in the way you speak the lines. Even though the play is far from naturalistic, as an actor you must prepare for it in much the same way as you would for a more conventional drama. For instance, what are the two characters' specific objectives in the scene? What are the actions (list them) and why are they carried out? Do you need to make use of emotional memory? If so, how would you go about it? What possible justifications are there for that bizarre, trancelike incantation before the stabbing? How would you convince an audience to accept it as possible, as frighteningly real? *The*

Lesson is fraught with questions and challenges like this.

2. Create a realistic situation, perhaps taken from experience, that parallels (but is less extreme than) the student-teacher relationship depicted in *The Lesson*. There can be one or many students. Play a teacher who deliberately cultivates and manipulates the attentions of an adoring flock, or play one of the disciples. Act out a classroom scene in which the teacher is obviously enjoying power for its own sake. Recall a teacher from your own past whose methods you believe to have been destructive, and impersonate him or her; exaggerate those methods until their shortcomings become painfully clear.

3. Those forty coffins have come to light, and the Professor is brought before a court (made up of the ghosts of his former students?). He tries to explain himself.

The learned astronomer, Clifford Hill, Gradgrind, M'Choakumchild, the Professor—it should be uncomfortably obvious by now that our store of texts comprises mostly negative examples of teachers and teaching. We are aware of this. Unfortunately, *good* teaching is not the stuff of drama—but much can be learned from studying the negative types. What makes for good teaching will be more and more apparent as the participants act out and exaggerate how *not* to teach. They will approach an understanding of effective teaching without being saddled with a set of inflexible formulae (the cookbook approach) on what to do in the classroom.

Still, lest you be left with a discouraging impression, we will add one more selection, taken from Maya Angelou's autobiography *I Know Why the Caged Bird Sings* (1970). Angelou, born Marguerite Johnson, describes at one point her childhood encounter with "the aristocrat" of the black community in Stamps, Arkansas: Mrs. Bertha Flowers, "the lady who threw me my first life line."[22] Angelou's experience does not take place in a classroom, and Mrs. Flowers' livelihood is not teaching. But their experience has much to do with what we have been talking about.

> There was a little path beside the rocky road, and Mrs. Flowers walked in front swinging her arms and picking her way over the stones.
>
> She said, without turning her head, to me, "I hear you're doing very good school work, Marguerite, but that it's all written. The teachers report that they have trouble getting you to talk in class." We passed the triangular farm on our left and the patch widened to allow us to walk together. I hung back in the separate unasked and unanswerable questions.
>
> "Come and walk along with me, Marguerite." I couldn't have refused even if I wanted to. She pronounced my name so nicely. Or more correctly, she spoke each word with such clarity that I was certain a foreigner who didn't understand English could have understood her.
>
> "Now no one is going to make you talk—possibly no one can. But bear in mind, language is man's way of communicating with his fellow man and it is language alone which separates him from the lower animals." That was a totally new idea to me, and I would need time to think about it.

[22]From *I Know Why the Caged Bird Sings,* by Maya Angelou. Copyright © 1969 by Maya Angelou, pp. 81–85. Reprinted by permission of Random House, Inc.

"Your grandmother says you read a lot. Every chance you get. That's good, but not good enough. Words mean more than what is set down on paper. It takes the human voice to infuse them with the shades of deeper meaning."

I memorized the part about the human voice infusing words. It seemed so valid and poetic.

She said she was going to give me some books and that I not only must read them, I must read them aloud. She suggested that I try to make a sentence sound in as many different ways as possible.

"I'll accept no excuse if you return a book to me that has been badly handled." My imagination boggled at the punishment I would deserve if in fact I did abuse a book of Mrs. Flowers'. Death would be too kind and brief.

The odors in the house surprised me. Somehow I had never connected Mrs. Flowers with food or eating or any other common experience of common people. There must have been an outhouse, too, but my mind never recorded it.

The sweet scent of vanilla had met us as she opened the door.

"I made tea cookies this morning. You see, I had planned to invite you for cookies and lemonade so we could have this little chat. The lemonade is in the icebox."

It followed that Mrs. Flowers would have ice on an ordinary day, when most families in our town bought ice late on Saturdays only a few times during the summer to be used in the wooden ice-cream freezers.

She took the bags from me and disappeared through the kitchen door. I looked around the room that I had never in my wildest fantasies imagined I would see. Browned photographs leered or threatened from the walls and the white, freshly done curtains pushed against themselves and against the wind. I wanted to gobble up the room entire and take it to Bailey, who would help me analyze and enjoy it.

"Have a seat, Marguerite. Over there by the table." She carried a platter covered with a tea towel. Although she warned that she hadn't tried her hand at baking sweets for some time, I was certain that like everything else about her the cookies would be perfect.

They were flat round wafers, slightly browned on the edges and butter-yellow in the center. With the cold lemonade they were sufficient for childhood's lifelong diet. Remembering my manners, I took nice little lady-like bites off the edges. She said she had made them expressly for me and that she had a few in the kitchen that I could take home to my brother. So I jammed one whole cake in my mouth and the rough crumbs scratched the insides of my jaws, and if I hadn't had to swallow, it would have been a dream come true.

As I ate she began the first of what we later called "my lessons in living." She said that I must always be intolerant of ignorance but understanding of illiteracy. That some people, unable to go to school, were more educated and even more intelligent than college professors. She encouraged me to listen carefully to what country people called mother wit. That in those homely sayings was couched the collective wisdom of generations.

When I finished the cookies she brushed off the table and brought a thick, small book from the bookcase. I had read *A Tale of Two Cities* and found it up to my standards as a romantic novel. She opened the first page and I heard poetry for the first time in my life.

"It was the best of times and the worst of times..." Her voice slid in and curved down through and over the words. She was nearly singing. I wanted to look at the pages. Were they the same that I had read? Or were there notes, music, lined on the pages, as in a hymn book? Her sounds began cascading gently. I knew from listening to a thousand preachers that she was nearing the end of her reading, and I hadn't really heard, heard to understand, a single word.

"How do you like that?"

It occurred to me that she expected a response. The sweet vanilla flavor was still on my tongue and her reading was a wonder in my ears. I had to speak.

I said, "Yes, ma'am." It was the least I could do, but it was the most also.

"There's one more thing. Take this book of poems and memorize one for me. Next time you pay me a visit, I want you to recite."

I have tried often to search behind the sophistication of years for the enchantment I so easily found in those gifts. The essence escapes but its aura remains. To be allowed, no, invited, into the private lives of strangers, and to share their joys and fears, was a chance to exchange the Southern bitter wormwood for a cup of mead with Beowulf or a hot cup of tea and milk with Oliver Twist. When I said aloud, "It is a far, far better thing that I do, than I have ever done . . ." tears of love filled my eyes at my selflessness.

On that first day, I ran down the hill and into the road (few cars ever came along it) and had the good sense to stop running before I reached the Store.

I was liked, and what a difference it made. I was respected not as Mrs. Henderson's grandchild or Bailey's sister but for just being Marguerite Johnson.

chapter twelve

Conclusion

After all of the generalizations and theoretical considerations, we need to come back to the practical experiences of those who have enrolled in our classes over the past several years.

One professor has taken to heart our advice about warm-ups. Before every lecture, he takes five minutes to do some quick exercises. That brief period of preparation helps him to focus on the presentational aspects of the lecture ahead: the energy level he will need, what movements will help, and how he will pace himself.

Two professors came to us in a quandary over the

question of humor. With too little humor, you eliminate the lightness that balances the seriousness of your subject matter and varies the day-to-day routine; too much humor, and you often lose the respect of your students and open the door for the class clowns to take over. The advice of Dr. Morris Burns (see chapter two) was helpful here. Although emphasizing the difficulty most actors have in cultivating a comic style (more difficult than what is typically required for tragedy), he does have one basic, helpful suggestion about humor and its use in the classroom: keep it light. First, keep abreast of your environment (current events, campus activities); second, learn as much as you can about the interests and concerns of your students. With this kind of awareness and information, as well as knowing when the right touch of humor is appropriate, the moments for spontaneous, humorous comment will come.

Some teachers and professors have come to us looking for major overhauls in their teaching, which students are not responding to at all. Again, much of what we advocate requires considerable time, feedback, and rehearsal in order to bear results. But we have been able to serve as a support group to begin the process. Consequently, these instructors have been able to make the critical first step towards improvement.

Many teachers have come to us knowing that they were already performing. In a sense, they were looking for validation of their established method (that what they were doing was sound pedagogically), as well as some formal introduction to the acting techniques they were already half-consciously using.

Finally, all who have undergone our training have done so with the realization that they could be better teachers. How many are there in our profession who will not even admit that possibility?

Our classmates have acknowledged that there is much the performer can say to the teacher about effective communication and motivation.

It is no coincidence that a book as important to actors as Stanislavski's *An Actor Prepares* should have as part of its title something so familiar to the teacher: the process of preparation. Unlike many other professionals, both actor and teacher are engaged in activities that call for a disproportionate amount of "behind-the-scenes" work; there is so much preparation that is necessary and yet quite invisible to those who are witnesses to the final product. Of course, the kinds of preparation are different. The actor is intent upon capturing just the right representation of a character who is built into an unvarying script, and he interacts with other performers, the set, and the audience. Lines must be memorized, too. Good teaching, on the other hand, has few requirements for exactitude of replication or memorization. Notes may be carried and referred to, and the script is changing all the time.

Still, both crafts depend on "overlearning" the lines or the lesson. The actor is then free to act, to "get out of the script." For many performers, the work of memorization is done well in advance: the creative work does not begin in earnest until they have the lines "down" so that they come automatically. Teachers too are at their best when they have "overlearned" their material and are able to move from behind that lectern and those notes and interact with students. Then they can field and answer questions comfortably; they can observe their students' faces and postures for clues about comprehension; they can readjust the lesson according to the class's response.

Both crafts also demand much in the way of spontaneity. The lecture that is read verbatim from start to finish is usually deadening; the part that is repeated mechanically every performance soon becomes a fossil. The best teaching, in fact, involves a downright flair for spontaneity in interpreting and individualizing the lesson for a particular class, with its particular mood and level of preparation in mind.

The benefits of energy are also common to both actors and teachers. Theater audiences and students alike attest to the value and the staying power of energetic performances. Ask people about their best teachers and you will hear descriptions like "enthusiastic," "dynamic," and "energetic." Ask teachers the same question and you will inevitably hear "a natural," "a thorough professional," and "dynamic." What both sets of responses have in common is this notion of energy, the value of which is hardly recognized in the training of teachers today.

Of course, "energy" is an elusive concept. It is a dynamic variable involving both actor and audience, teacher and class in a complex and fragile relationship. It is an interactive process in which the participants feed and sustain each other, moving the performance or lesson into higher and higher realms. The psychological "rush" accompanying a performance that is really exciting to an audience can produce even higher levels of energy in the performer. For teachers, the highs are not as intense but still possible. A class that gets "cooking" is the ultimate stimulus for most teachers, providing the kind of reinforcement that often allows them to withstand all the other hassles involved.

There is also the element of psychological renewal for the instructor. Even the most venerable of professors must teach the same material on a fairly regular basis. How can that content be kept fresh? One answer is to look for different ways to make the material come to life. Each semester, a different component could be dramatized or enlivened in some way. Furthermore, by moving toward the process of induction and discovery, teachers can never be sure of where their students will be heading. Hence comes the continuing challenge.

Remember, though, that the effects of performance skills are by no means limited to the teacher. For the student, the teacher's efforts toward dramatization in the classroom provide numerous psychological advantages. First, an emotional prod is established, which can help to organize and later recall cognitive information. The effects of dramatization both secure attention and aid memory. Second, an important element of variety is introduced, which also helps to maintain the students' attention. Third, a climate of risk is established; the instructor accepts the challenges of producing exciting theatrics and hopes that these will extend to the students themselves taking risks and becoming more active learners. Finally, performance-oriented teaching encourages discovery and inductive learning. Solutions are not always spelled out by the instructor, but rather are left to the students to explore. An accurate representation of the event is presented much like an original source. Students are dissuaded from accepting the easy conclusions of secondary sources and are encouraged instead to

Figure 14. Coauthor Dr. William Timpson, shown with his daughter Kellee, says, "There is no finer performer than a two-year-old."

come up with their own interpretations.[23]

The authors of this book come from different academic disciplines (education and English literature) and different teaching experiences. From the beginning of our collaboration—a lecture on teachers in literature for an undergraduate education class—we have been acutely aware of the complexity and scope of this new field, teaching as performing. There is more that we need to learn, and there is certainly more than can be covered in one book. Still, beginnings are necessary, however tentative and incomplete.

[23]The writings of Jean Piaget and Jerome Bruner come quickly to mind; so does the preschool program developed by Maria Montessori. See Piaget, *The Origins of Intelligence in Children,* trans. Margaret Cook (New York: International University Press, 1952); Bruner, *Toward a Theory of Instruction* (Cambridge, Mass.: Harvard University Press, 1966); and E. M. Standing, *The Montessori Revolution in Education* (New York: Schocken Books, 1966).

We remain convinced that the more teachers there are who see themselves as bona fide members of the performance guild, the more people are going to learn. It is that simple.

appendix

Related Programs

Performance possibilities in the classroom are being explored more and more. The methods of Professor John Rassias clearly demonstrate the pedagogical validity of "teaching as performing," while other programs have been developed that emphasize the value of performance for students. In this appendix, we summarize the work of several different approaches that have been demonstrably successful. They all bring the performing arts and the classroom closer together.

THE RASSIAS METHOD

The "Dartmouth Intensive Language Model," developed by John Rassias, Professor of Foreign Languages at Dartmouth College, has drawn considerable attention in this country, and not just in educational circles.[24] Making use of a frenetic pace and all kinds of dramatic techniques (impersonation, physical and vocal variety, etc.), the guiding master teacher goes through the pronunciation of new material, helps with grammar, and clears up any problems with the lesson of the day. Then the class (no more than twenty-two) splits into two groups and spends another fifty minutes with an apprentice teacher: an undergraduate trained in "the Rassias method." After this, the students move to language lab, where there is more practice with another apprentice. Central to this method is the theatrical illustration of new words and expressions, since the only language which can be spoken in class is the language being taught. Because each student is expected to speak sixty-five times per fifty-minute session, pacing is also critical; apprentice teachers must keep the class hustling. There is no homework expected outside of class time.

Rassias believes that traditional language programs place far too much emphasis on vocabulary and pronunciation. He pushes his students instead to have the courage to speak, using all the enthusiasm he can muster to break down their inhibitions. He will, for instance, put on the costume (wig and all) of an

[24]See Stan Luxenberg, "All the Class a Stage," in "Report on Teaching No. 5," *Change* 10 (1978):30–33; and Richard Wolkomir, "A Manic Professor Tries to Close Up the Language Gap," *Smithsonian,* May 1980, pp. 80–86.

eighteenth-century French philosopher in order to explain a work to an advanced class in French literature. Some of the gestures he has used to make points include cracking an egg on the head of one student, bear-hugging another, and mock-strangling a third. In this way he breaks down inhibitions about failure but carefully avoids humiliating his sometimes bewildered audience.

His students also get into the act. New York City transit policemen, who were in one of Rassias's classes to learn Spanish, found themselves acting out a scene in an imaginary subway station. A heart-attack victim lay on the platform, two men were picking his pockets, and a crowd watched in silence. The policemen had to deal with the situation in Spanish. Other classes have developed skits (complete with props and special effects) that lead to a greater facility with the language.

Rassias himself studied to be a French teacher but found that his enthusiasm for the language was lost on his students. He turned to the theater, earning a doctorate in drama and acting professionally in Paris. He still thought of teaching, however, and eventually moved toward a style that used performance skills to improve communication. He returned to the University of Bridgeport as a language instructor, eager to merge his theatrical experience with his teaching. The Peace Corps asked for his help in improving its language offerings, and he was able to experiment in a grand way. Out of this came the Dartmouth Intensive Language Model. It has been so successful that the method is now used in the teaching of all languages at Dartmouth, as well as at more than thirty-eight other schools.

SUGGESTOPEDIA

Another program that works involves something called "suggestopedia." Interestingly enough, the context is again the foreign-language class, and the objective is to break down the typical anxieties that students bring to language learning. Central to this technique is setting the proper mood. In a manner resembling the way opening acts are employed to "warm up" an audience, time is taken at the beginning of each class period to relax and focus. The instructor takes the students through several relaxation exercises, alternately tightening and relaxing various muscle groups from the head down to the feet. Students move to a more relaxed state, and with eyes shut they can focus on the beauties of the language and the countries where it is spoken. Thus the term suggestopedia: the value of each lesson is *suggested* to the students at the outset.

CREATIVE DRAMATICS

Creative Dramatics for the Classroom Teacher, by Ruth Heinig and Lyda Stillwell, is a practical guide and a good introduction to another adaptation of theater to the classroom, this one primarily for students:

> Creative dramatics involves informal drama experiences. These may include pantomimes, improvised stories and skills, movement activities and exploration, and dramatic songs and games. The experiences are planned by the children under the guidance of a teacher.

The purpose of creative dramatics is for the growth and development of the players rather than for the entertainment of an audience. Plays may be created by the children, but the action and dialogue are improvised rather than memorized from written scripts. The only written scripts that might be considered are those that the children write *after* they have improvised a scene and wish to *record* what they have created.[25]

The authors describe documented benefits of creative dramatics: improved language arts skills through stimulating demands for communication; improved problem-solving and social skills through requirements for cooperative efforts; stimulation of creative imagination; and a deeper understanding of human behavior. Creative dramatics has also been used therapeutically to give vent to emotional tensions. But perhaps most important, it has meant fun and participation in the classroom.

Advocates of creative dramatics claim that it is a superb means of translating abstract concepts into experiences that young children especially can relate to kinesthetically. Also, students learn to identify and empathize with others. They develop an ability to take multiple perspectives, a key skill if an education is to be truly multicultural.

Like teachers who realize the value of performing skills, students will also come to know themselves, others, and their environment better through the study of movement and performance. Creative dramatics demands an involvement in the learning process

[25]Ruth Heinig and Lyda Stillwell, *Creative Dramatics for the Classroom Teacher* (Englewood Cliffs, N.J.: Prentice-Hall, Inc., 1974), pp. 5–6. Reprinted by permission of the publisher.

that forces students to become active and responsible. It also provides structured outlets for students' initiative and energy.

Examples of activities in creative dramatics include:

1. For elementary students: "finger plays" of stories, poems or songs. As they recite, children use their fingers, hands, or entire bodies to act out what is being said. For instance:

Hickory, Dickory, Dock	(Arms and hands clasped, swaying like a pendulum)
The mouse ran up the clock	(Fingers run quickly upwards)
The clock struck one	(Hold up index finger)
The mouse ran down	(Fingers run quickly downwards)
Hickory, Dickory, Dock	(Repeat first motion)

2. Single-action poetry. Since much poetry involves movement both in the images conveyed and the meter itself, elementary-school children can perform the action—running, galloping, hopping—at their desks, seated or standing. Longfellow's "Paul Revere's Ride" is one possibility.

3. Action songs. Students of all ages can really enliven a song by adding some theatrics or movements to it. "Michael, Row the Boat Ashore" has such possibilities.

4. Action games. "Follow the Leader" and "Simon Says" are two good examples of excellent warm-ups and icebreakers for any group activity.

5. Action stories. Again, students of all ages can be

involved in dramatizations of stories, whether they be published works or stories written by students.

6. Games that build sensory and communicative skills. If teachers want to incorporate any of these ideas, some attention and effort will have to be given to developing the skills students will need. As we advise teachers to become more aware of themselves and their craft, so students will also need help. Sensory games focus on seeing, hearing, tasting, smelling, and touching; they build observational and expressive abilities. Communication games focus on increasing speaking, listening, and cooperating skills.

7. Pantomime. Teachers must learn to communicate more effectively though nonverbal modes; students can learn to benefit from this as well. Greater self-awareness, physical flexibility, and expressiveness are all important objectives of pantomime. Actions or stories can be recited for all to pantomime. Direction and tempo can be varied (right, left, forward, back, up, down; fast, normal, or slow motion). Feelings can be explored (frustration, sympathy, concentration, energy, the blahs). Conflicts and resolutions can be demonstrated (homework assignments vs. a favorite T.V. show; career ambition vs. surviving a rotten required class; approaching the unapproachable vs. getting that special date). Creative challenges can also be posed and nontraditional, expansive thinking encouraged: the mouse that roared, a hot "cool," an energetic daze, well-conditioned fat, impulsive perseverance.

8. The enactment of characters and events out of history, modern times, or literature. This is really a capstone activity, built upon all of the preceding, which allows students of all ages to become personally involved through dramatization. Characters and events must be thoroughly researched, ideas and conflicts explored, and their representation experimented with. The most important and enduring value here may lie in your encouragement of this as active learning.

9. Finally, quieting activities. Once all this creativity has been unleashed, it is important that energies be quieted and refocused for the rest of the school day. Students can enact a quiet poem or song with eyes closed, or visual images could be used as a guide for relaxation (for example, a candle burning and the wax slowly dripping down).

MOVEMENT ACTIVITIES

Peter Werner and Elsie Burton, in *Learning through Movement,* express goals similar to those of creative dramatics and extol the benefits of active learning through a multisensory and enjoyable approach. The authors claim that movement involves the psychomotor domain in exploring cognitive and affective areas. The younger the child, the more essential this becomes. Werner and Burton state:

> Learning through movement is the oldest teaching method. Among primitive people, one's education consisted of learning how to physically survive. In time the pendulum swung from a system that was entirely

physical to one that was purely intellectual. Gradually educators have come to realize that intelligence permeates all human activity and that it is inseparably interrelated with emotions, social interaction, and physical activity. This realization fostered the development of teaching methods that combine mental and physical activity.[26]

Today's children, overwhelmed by electronic media, are information-rich and action-poor. Television means passivity. Using movement as an aid for learning, the authors say, will counteract this tendency in many ways:

1. Children will attend to their classroom assignments better.

2. Students are also provided with an experiential, physical base for new concepts.

3. Schooling generally is enhanced through greater enjoyment of the learning process.

4. Action-centered learning will also partially compensate for learning disabilities, limitations, or styles that interfere with a unisensory, cognitive approach.

5. Participation and involvement are encouraged.

Here are some examples of activities involving movement given by Werner and Burton. Although these activities and those of creative dramatics have been developed with primary-grade children, there is

[26]Peter Werner and Elsie Burton, *Learning through Movement* (St. Louis: C. V. Mosby Co., 1979), p. 1.

potential for adaptive use at the secondary level. Take some risks and experiment.

General

- Developing better listening skills through activities and games such as "Simon Says." Students are notoriously poor listeners when they are communicating among themselves; notice the interactions when students lead a discussion.

- Involving students and enhancing enjoyment through creative storytelling. Again, we are appealing to the active learner as well as the student who could benefit from a multisensory approach.

- Reinforcement for language-decoding activities: students physically act out letters, sounds, words, or expressions, or "hop out" the letters of a word on a floor letter chart. These kinds of activities would help many young readers and spellers as well as anyone attempting to learn a second language.

- Building communication skills. Giving and receiving directions for a physical activity or game require a degree of explicitness and clarity that students often have difficulty with.

- Nonverbal communicative exercises, which help students learn how to express their feelings nonverbally and thereby better monitor themselves.

Mathematics

- Hopping out arithmetic problems on a floor number chart

- Making the shape of numbers for answering
- Exploring number or set theory through physical groups
- Making conversions into metrics of distances run, walked, or jumped
- Forming geometric shapes and exploring their properties
- Exploring graphs with human configurations

Science

- Exploring the concept of stability: balance while still or moving, with differing bases of support or centers of gravity
- Exploring the concept of leverage: seesawing, moving objects of differing dimensions, using pulleys, playing tug of war
- Exploring Newton's laws of motion: jumping, bouncing a ball, moving mass through distance
- Exploring concepts of energy and force, resistance, friction, motion, centripetal and centrifugal force
- Exploring the nature of sound
- Utilizing movements in other sciences (biological, earth, physical)

Social Studies

- Learning to live, work, and play together through physical activities

- Exploring personal space
- Dramatizing machines and assembly lines

History and Multicultural Education

- Dances and games of various ethnic groups and nations
- Holiday celebrations and traditions

Music and Art

- Rhythmic activities (tempo, beat, accent, meter, rests, even and uneven rhythms)
- Exploring musical concepts like melody, pitch, dynamics, and form
- Exploring art concepts and forms: body and spatial awareness, design and composition, shape, and form

Index